When Your Baby Dies

Whether your child is a newborn, or age sixty, he or she will always be your baby.

Renee Hogan Blythe

When Your Baby Dies

An Inspirational Journey of Grief

iUniverse, Inc.
Bloomington

WHEN YOUR BABY DIES
AN INSPIRATIONAL JOURNEY OF GRIEF

iUniverse books may be ordered through booksellers or by contacting:

iUniverse
1663 Liberty Drive
Bloomington, IN 47403
www.iuniverse.com
1-800-Authors (1-800-288-4677)

Because of the dynamic nature of the Internet, any web addresses or links contained in this book may have changed since publication and may no longer be valid. The views expressed in this work are solely those of the author and do not necessarily reflect the views of the publisher, and the publisher hereby disclaims any responsibility for them.

Any people depicted in stock imagery provided by Thinkstock are models, and such images are being used for illustrative purposes only.

Certain stock imagery © Thinkstock.

ISBN: 978-1-4759-7917-6 (sc)
ISBN: 978-1-4759-7916-9 (hc)
ISBN: 978-1-4759-7915-2 (e)

Library of Congress Control Number: 2013903912

Printed in the United States of America

iUniverse rev. date: 4/12/2013

IN MEMORY OF MY SON

KRISTOPHER GLEN HARDRICK
December 15, 1977 – June 3, 2008

PORTRAIT OF KRIS

Table of Contents

●●●●●●●●●●●●●●●●●●●●●●●●●●●●●●●●●●●

THE CORD

●·●

We are connected…
My child and I,
By an invisible cord, not seen by the eye
It is not the cord that connects us at birth
This cord cannot been seen by anyone on Earth
This cord does the work right from the start
It binds us together…Attached to the heart
I know it is there, though no one can see…
The invisible cord from my child to me
The strength of this cord is hard to describe
It cannot be destroyed
It cannot be denied
It is stronger than any cord Man could create
It withstands the test
Can hold any weight
And though you are gone,
And, you are not here with me
The cord is still here…But no one can see
It pulls at my heart
I am bruised
I am sore
But this cord is my lifeline… As never before
I am thankful that God connects a mother and child this way
With an invisible cord death cannot take away

Author Unknown

INTRODUCTION

This book is for the living. I wrote my book for grieving parents living in a cold world of people who have a difficult time understanding the shock and devastation we (the parents) experience from the death of a child. Especially, for those who have experienced the loss of an only child.

Even though, I chose the title *When Your Baby Dies* for personal reasons, I want my readers to know I wrote my book to help parents who have lost a child at any age and by any means, including by accident, SIDS, murder, suicide, at birth, illness or from natural causes. I believe whether your child is a newborn or age sixty he or she will *always* be your baby.

I personally lost my only child, Kristopher at the age of thirty. He died on June 3, 2008. With no warning, his heart stopped in his sleep and autopsy determined *Natural Causes*.

I searched for books on grief after my loss and found few on the loss of children. I think living the grief experience is so hard that parents cannot bring themselves to write about it.

Personally, I started writing my book in 2008, shortly after the death of my son and set it aside.

I found it was difficult to write about my journey of grief when I had just begun the experience it for myself.

Now, with five years of this grief journey behind me, I feel confident my experience can help some parents know that the things they feel after the death of their child are normal.

I am not a medical professional, a spiritualist, psychic or journalist. I am a mother who had her only child die at a young age. This is my own personal story written with the spiritual guidance of God.

Many people may have different opinions about the topics discussed. I convey to the readers my personal opinions and feelings. They are welcome to disagree.

I believe there is no right way or wrong way to grieve. There is no right way or wrong way to worship. It is a journey each and every one of us must travel in one's own way with no limits on time. My intensions are to help parents through the grief journey, so that their experience may be a little easier and hopefully a little faster than my own.

My goal is to help parents who have lost a child in death to know that they are not alone. There are millions of us.

I am grateful that I can now express to others that there is a light at the end of the dark path we are traveling, and a road of recovery that can lead us to a place where we learn to live a *new normal*.

I pray that parents find solace in reading *When Your Baby Dies*.

Renee Hogan Blythe - Author

CHAPTER 1
THE LIGHT OF MY LIFE

On December 15, 1977, in a small county hospital in Arkansas my son, Kristopher Glen Hardrick, made his grand entrance into this world. Robert, Kris's father, and me were thankful for the birth of this beautiful, healthy son.

Robert was a good looking man. He had large, brown eyes, thick brown hair and a muscular body. His beautiful smile could warm your heart every time.

I was an outgoing young, brunette, woman full of life. My big, blue eyes were shining when they placed Kris in my arms that day. An overwhelming feeling of *pure love* engulfed my every sense.

As a young girl, I always felt something was missing from me. I had feelings of nobody loving me. I cannot explain why. I had loving parents who worked hard to give me and my two brothers everything we needed or wanted. I believe this feeling has been with me since birth for some strange reason.

Kris changed all of that for me. On the day of my son's birth, I knew in my heart that he would love me just the way that I love my mom. Having a baby to love and someone to love me made me happier than anything ever had in my life.

Robert and I were both determined to make sure this baby

had all that he needed to get through life just as both parents had done for us. We made those commitments to each other.

When we met, I fell in love with Robert at first sight. We spent time traveling together for a couple of years before we married, and we had lots of plans for the future, which included much more travel.

Only two weeks after we married I found out I was pregnant. Robert was not happy about it, but he did eventually come around and seem happier after the birth of Kris.

My marriage to Robert was short lived. We divorced when Kris was eighteen months old. He was not happy being still and raising a family. He wanted to leave us for his home state of Georgia and do some traveling on his own.

Robert was never a part of mine and Kris's lives after he left, with the exception of one short visit Kris had with him when he was fifteen years old. Before then, he did not call Kris. He did not pay child support. He just did not care. It is that simple.

Kris and I had many ups and downs after his father left us as all families do I suppose, but even under difficult circumstances, we always had each other. I would say to Kris "It's you and me against the world—just the two of us."

Kris would say looking up at me with those big, brown eyes "Just you and me Mom."

Kris got many of his father's traits—his good looks, billiard skills, artistic skills and facial expressions. He got my intelligence and kind heart. He was always willing to offer a helping hand to someone in need and less fortunate than himself. Financially, neither one of us could help people much, but we could buy them a meal or give them a warm place to sleep if they needed it.

In 1987, Kris and I moved from Arkansas to Virginia Beach, Virginia. Kris was nine years old. This was a huge move for us. We found ourselves in a big city, and neither of us knew anyone.

This move only helped to bring me and Kris closer to each

other. We spent time together playing on the beach, watching the sunset over the ocean, going to ballgames, eating out, just whatever we could find to do for fun.

I found a new job in sales and marketing with good benefits and salary. The first friend I made in Virginia was Janet. Janet is a beautiful slender blonde with blue eyes and a bubbly personality. She was pregnant with her first child. We worked and rode to and from work together every day for over one year. Janet and her husband included Kris and I in many activities and we became close over the years, like family.

Another friend I made in Virginia Beach was with Doris Ann. Doris is part Cherokee Indian with dark black, curly hair, a slender body and brown eyes. She was an insurance agent for many years. She came to work where I was working about one year after I moved here.

Doris and I have always been hangout buddies. We worked together, went out together, lived together for about three months, and talked every day. She knew all of my secrets. It took some time, but Kris and I finally got established in the new city.

My Kris worshiped me. He thought I was the best mom in the world. He talked about me to everyone he met. He would tell them, "My Mom is so smart, and one of the strongest women I have ever known," usually referring to the ups and downs we had during this life together.

He would go on to tell them how I taught him to dance and got him into loving rock n' roll and country music all at the same time; and how he got me into Bob Marley and taught me to dance *Rasta*.

I have heard Kris say, "My Mom taught me how to clean house and cook so that I did not need to depend on a woman." He would giggle and roll his eyes when he said that. In reality, cleaning the house was the way he earned his allowance.

Kris told stories about how productive he thought I was in sales and how I taught him to be a good salesperson.

He loved to draw from the time he was a small boy. He started drawing the figures of *He-Man* and *Skeletor* when he was in the second grade. Kris became accomplished in drawing most anything he saw. He drew portraits well. Although Kris did not pursue a career in art, he maintained his love of art his entire life.

My son owned a custom painting company he named Extraordinary Painting with the slogan *I Do The Extras Ordinary Painters Don't*. By the age of twenty eight, Kris had become quite a man, and he had just begun to get focused on making life good for him; and for me.

Kris looked so much like his father after he grew up. I can remember thinking many times how much he reminded me of Robert. His expressions were almost identical to his father's. He had the same muscular body, the same brown eyes, and the same thick brown hair. Kris was even flat footed like his father. It was almost scary how many of his father's traits Kris had without ever being around him.

Kris would say, "Mom just wait, one of these days I am going to buy you everything, and you deserve the best. I am going to buy you a new home, a new car and take care of you, just like you have taken care of me."

I would say, "You just concentrate on taking care of you and that will be good enough for me."

My birthday is on May 28th. My birthday always falls during the Memorial Day week which makes it hard to celebrate because so many people make plans for the holiday. I usually found something to do, but many times Kris and I spent my birthday together and celebrated alone.

He got a kick out of baking me a birthday cake and decorating it, and I could count on a homemade card. If he did buy a birthday card, he would always include a drawing of his own with a special message written inside just for me.

In 2008, Kris bought me a 2005 Jeep Grand Cherokee for my birthday. This was the first substantial gift he had ever purchased for me. Kris was so proud of himself. The Jeep was not brand new, but it looked new and it had all of the extras with low mileage. He was just beaming when he handed me the keys that day. I found myself in shock that my son had went out and bought me a vehicle.

Kris had been driving my 1998 Ford Ranger that I won in a sales contest ten years earlier. My Mercedes had broken down leaving me without transportation. Kris felt guilty because he was using my truck for his business and I was driving an old Jimmy I purchased for four hundred dollars.

He said the day he gave me the Jeep, "Here's the deal Mom I am buying you the Cherokee, but the Ranger is mine."

I gave him a loving smile, hugged him and agreed. The Ranger was his anyway, but I had not told him. He took better care of the truck thinking it was mine.

I have so many delightful memories of Kris and those memories will *never* die. Memories are more cherished than we think. I do know this today.

I can remember one year at Christmas Kris bought me a beautiful, leather sculpture of a Native American Indian. I loved it. My home had a Native American Indian decor, and I had many collectables.

About two weeks later a knock came at the door, and a lady was standing there with this package and asked me, "Do you have a son named Kris?"

I said, "Yes."

With a big smile, she handed me this heavy package and replied, "Your son was trying to carry this gift on a bicycle. He appeared to be having a difficult time, so I offered to deliver it for him."

I thanked her and offered to pay her, and she said in a pleasant voice, "No, I volunteered to help him," and left.

Kris had bought me an original concrete sculpture done by Native American Indian children. It was truly original. I called him and thanked him and commented that he should not spend his money on me like that. His comment back was, "Well mom, you plan to leave everything to me, right?"

I laughed and said, "I see you are just hoarding your inheritance!" It was a fun day.

Kris loved to cook. Yes, he was my master chef! My mom gave him a summer job one year at age fifteen cooking in a Biscuitville breakfast restaurant, in the state of North Carolina. My dad was fighting to survive leukemia and Kris went to help them out for almost one year.

Kris loved working in the restaurant business. He continued to work as a cook in several of the restaurants in Virginia Beach after he came back home. He could cook a fantastic breakfast. Some of the fascinating recipes he created on his own, I still use today.

It was a barbeque every weekend with Kris around. He would come in with bags of groceries on Friday evening and say, "I work hard for my money and I plan to eat well." He always made sure everyone in the house got steak, crab legs, ribs, just whatever he chose to cook. He had a generous heart and never minded sharing the fruits of his labor.

His favorite channels on television were the History channel and the Discovery channel. He would spend hours watching history on Hitler and stories of the Masons or predictions of the end of time.

Not long after the 911 incident, somebody painted a swastika on a huge, oak tree in the front yard. Kris came in from work and said, "Did you see that big Nazi sign on our tree?"

I said, "Yes," and rolled my eyes. He took some spray paint and tried to change it to look like an American flag. Then he set out to find who did this to the tree.

He found them too. It was two eleven year old boys. He visited their homes, and in front of their parents Kris gave them each an hour lecture on Hitler.

I thought that was so funny and appropriate for what they had done.

Maybe two years later a police officer knocked on my door and asked me about the painting on the tree. I explained what had happened, and he said, "You can file a complaint and have something done about this."

I told him, "It's been awhile since it happened and my son found the two young children who did this and he gave them a long lecture on Hitler, so I believe they have both been punished."

The police officer hesitantly replied, "Well if you think so."

I said, "You do not know my son," and laughed.

In 2004, I wanted to add color to my interior walls, so I asked Kris to paint them for me. He painted some accent walls in a bedroom and the dining room and living room, painted my office yellow and repainted all of the trim in my house. The paint job turned out lovely. Kris is quite a perfectionist when it comes to his painting work.

One night, he was drinking some beer and pulled out all of the colors of paint he used when painting the interior and painted a giant mural on my living room wall. I was not sure I was going to like it. He said, "Mom, this is my first mural and I want to do it." So I agreed.

Today, I would not take a million dollars for that mural. It is priceless to me. A picture of my mural is at the end of this chapter.

I could go on for hours about the fantastic memories I have of Kris. There are many stories I would love to tell everyone, but mainly I need people to know Kristopher Hardrick was a marvellous person. He existed in every way possible for me.

I never want Kris to be forgotten. I pray I have offered everyone just a small glimpse of his life with his mom. He was, and he still is *the light of my life*.

WALL MURAL

CHAPTER 2
THE OBITUARY

● ●

It was a Monday morning in June, and I was doing some paperwork for the swimming pool company in my home. Six days earlier I had a fractured rib and working outdoors in the sun was not the place I needed to be at the time. My business partner and roommate, Frank was doing the pool work that we had scheduled for the day.

Frank is a hard working man who had a dream of owning his own business; so together we had spent the past year building a small swimming pool business to help earn us a comfortable income. We had just started the second pool season in the summer of 2008.

Frank is a native of Virginia Beach. He is a six foot, balding man with brown eyes and strong body. He is an extremely confident man in most everything he does.

Frank has worked in the pool and concrete business since he was sixteen years old. He has also worked in many of the high end restaurants here and I consider him a skilful cook. He and Kris would have cooking contests.

At the time, the desktop computer in my office had a virus, so I was using the computer in my son's room. Kris came in at lunch to surprise me with two large sub sandwiches.

I suggested we share one of the subs because they were way

too large for me to eat one alone. Kris said excitedly, "Great that will leave me one to eat when I come home." My son loved to cook, and loved to eat.

Kris asked me, "Did you see the chicken marinating in the fridge?"

I said, "No, I do not think I have even been to the refrigerator today."

He said, "No big deal; I just wanted you to know I am cooking tonight, so you do not have too."

"I appreciate that son because I am not feeling well" I replied lovingly.

And cook, he did! He cooked, chicken, mashed potatoes, corn on the cob, green beans and slaw. It all tasted delightful. Kris, Frank and I talked and joked around some and just had a good evening meal together.

Around 9:30 that evening I went to the bathroom and Kris was lying on the couch watching Discovery. I stopped and looked over at him and said, "Thank you for cooking son, it tasted so good."

He said, "You're welcome Mom" in his sweet cheerful voice.

Later, about midnight, Kris came into my room and asked for some Nyquil. He said, "I have a monster day tomorrow and I cannot sleep. Maybe Nyquil will help."

He took a drink of Nyquil and left my room. I had no idea those were the last words I would hear my precious son say to me.

At 3:30 a.m. I went to the bathroom and noticed Kris was sleeping soundly on the couch. I thought to myself Kris is sleeping sound; the Nyquil must have worked for him. Then around 7:30 a.m., I went to the bathroom, and he was still asleep on the couch.

This was unusual since most of the time he was up getting his lunch made, and getting ready to head out for a day of work at that time of the morning. I thought to myself while in the bathroom, I better wake him, or he will be mad at me for letting him oversleep.

As I walked over to him, a feeling came over me, and I thought, it seems like he was in the same position earlier this morning.

I got to the couch and softly patted his face and said, "Son did you oversleep?"

He did not respond. Then I felt of his arm, and it was chilly, but we had a window air conditioner, so I thought not much of that.

Next, I walked to the end of the couch and felt his foot sticking out from under the blanket, and I shook it and said, "Kris wake up!"

His foot felt hard and then I tried to take the remote control out of his hand, and the remote stuck in his hand.

I started screaming, "*Oh No God! Please, Please! No, God! Please! No, God! Please! Please! Please!*"

I went to him and laid my head on his chest; and cried; and kissed him on the face; and begged him to wake up, but I knew he had passed on from my world. At that second, a heavy *fog* engulfed me.

I ran back into my room and woke Frank and said "Help me my baby is dead!"

Frank ran to the living room and checked Kris's pulse and he started jumping up and down and crying and saying, "No God, not again."

Frank is not his father but he loved Kris, and he became terribly upset. In 1981, Frank's brother died from an accident. He was hit by a car on his bicycle at the age of fifteen. I am sure those old memories came back to him that morning.

I went to the phone and called 911 and said, "Please come quick to ____ New York Avenue, my baby is dead!"

The dispatch lady said, "How old is your baby?"

"He is thirty", I told her.

"Please hurry," and I hung up the phone.

Next, I called my mom and told her Kris had died, and I was crying uncontrollably, so Frank had to take the phone to finish the conversation with Mom. Frank said, "Your mom is going to contact your brothers and the rest of the family for you, so you do not have to call them."

The third call was to Greg, another roommate. Greg is a close friend who rents a room from me. He had lived with Kris and me for over four years. He is a balding Irish man from Ohio who works as a floor mechanic.

I met Greg in 1991. He and Kris were *garage buddies* and had become close friends. They both liked their rock and roll music and cold beer. After I told Greg that Kris had died, he came home from work immediately.

Next, I called my two best friends Janet and Doris, to ask them to please come be by my side. Janet was here before the coroner left. She kept me calm because the police wanted to call it a crime scene! This upset me because it was quite obvious that Kris died peacefully. He had the remote control in his hand!

Next, I had to interview with the police officer in charge in private about what had happened the night before and he questioned me about drugs and alcohol and any medical conditions that Kris had. He was much kinder to me than the other police officers in my house. I was so glad I did not have to get ugly with him.

The same officer spoke to Frank before he left for court that morning and called the court to inform them that we had a death in the home. He also interviewed Greg after he spoke to Frank.

Doris arrived about an hour after I called her. She lives about forty miles from me and she was emotional because she as Janet, had known Kris since he was ten years old. Doris and Janet both were here with me every day until the funeral was over.

My family lived five hours away close to Charlotte, North

Carolina. I received calls immediately from my two brothers Tim, and Tony to let me know they were on their way.

Tim is four years younger than I am and he has a girlfriend named Jenita. He works as a welder and iron worker, and he has one son, Chancey, who lives in Arkansas. I have always called Tim *my little big brother* because he has a size 27" waist and he wears a size 14 boy's shirt at the age of fifty. Tim has dark hair and blue eyes. He reminds me of Randy Owens in the Alabama band. He has one grandchild by the name of Haley, age five, and a grandson on the way.

Tony is my youngest brother or *my big little brother* as I call him. He and his wife Janet have six beautiful children, Leslie, Anthony, Byron, Randi, Brandon and Brittney. His trade is pipe fitting, and Janet owns an *Ebay* store.

Tony is 5"10 and weighs about 300 pounds. He looks a lot like me and with brown hair and blue eyes, and he is solid like a rock.

At the time, Tony and Janet had one grandchild by the name of Jenny. They now have four grandchildren, Jenny, Gracie, Trevor and Gage.

My mother is a tall slender woman with a warm smile and salt and pepper hair. She has beautiful blue eyes, and she is extremely attractive for a senior in her seventies.

My daddy was a carpenter. He was a stout Irish and Native American Indian man with blue eyes and strong muscles. He worked all of the time, from sunrise to sundown. Daddy planted a sizeable garden every year to help feed us and worked in the construction field most of his life.

He loved to hunt and fish and spend his time in the great outdoors. Daddy showed me how to do so many things before he died from cancer in February of 1999. *I have written a poem and dedicated it to my daddy at the end of this chapter.*

Mom remarried on May 9, 2008 to Phil, a man she dated for about three years after my father died. Phil had never met my son, but he found himself quickly thrown in the middle of

13

one of the families biggest tragedies. He is a tall thin gray haired man with a strong country accent and he enjoys talking.

At 8:30 a.m. Frank had to leave me with Janet, Greg and the police and go to the courthouse. My house was a wreck because Kris had just cooked a large meal and left the dishes. We were in the middle of the busy swimming pool season, and I had not taken the time to do much house cleaning. Suddenly, I found myself facing the reality that many people would be coming to my home.

I called some more friends in the cleaning business and asked for their immediate help getting my house ready for guests. Sylvia and her family came to the house right away with the cleaning supplies in hand to help me. The carpet cleaning company was there within one hour. I was so grateful for their kindness.

Next, I had to tell Patty, my son's girlfriend of three years that Kris was dead. She had been calling his phone all morning, and we did not answer because she had just lost her mom in April of 2008. I did not want her to come to my house until the coroner had left with Kris.

Patty is a fragile sweet lady. She was a few years older than Kris, but she loved him immensely. She is petite with brown hair and blue eyes with a sweet helpful nature.

When I did eventually answer his phone, Patty asked, "Did Kris leave his phone at home again?"

I told her, "No he did not leave it home."

She asked me with concern, "What is wrong then?; I'm coming over there."

I explained politely to her, "You should wait and come over in about one hour Patty."

She said again, "Okay what is wrong?"

"Just come over in an hour we will talk then." I replied.

Telling Patty Kris had died was one of the hardest things I had to do. She totally lost it and started saying, "I should have been here! I could have saved him!"

I tried to comfort her, but I did not know how. We both just held each other and cried and cried and cried.

It is an absolute fact that every minute has been hard from the moment I realized my son was dead to this very day.

Kris's father, Robert had died in November of 2007. We found out on Christmas Day when I did a *Google* search of Kris's name. Robert's obituary popped up on *Google*. When I told Kris his father was dead, he did not cry. He said, "I wonder if he had any regrets about how he treated me my entire life, and if he left me at least a piece of pool chalk?"

I personally contacted Robert's sister after we found out he had died and she talked to Kris. She told him that Robert did try to get in touch with him before he died from liver disease, but he could not find a working phone number for us. I am sure Robert did not know my last name.

Robert's wife did send Kris a few things that belonged to his father through the mail. Her kindness made Kris feel better.

Later that morning, I started receiving one phone call after another phone call. A call from the coroner's office about the autopsy, a call from LifeNet Health about Kris being a donor and calls from the funeral homes, friends, family and of course the pool calls for the business.

It is funny, but those pool calls taught me a powerful lesson in life. Most people simply *do not care* what has happened in your life. I would answer my phone and say, "I am sorry, but my son died this morning unexpectedly and you will need to call Frank at this phone number about your pool, I cannot take calls right now." Many of them would keep on insisting that I talk to them!

I would get angry and say to them, "Excuse me, did you understand what I just said to you? My son died this morning unexpectedly."

They would say, "Yes, I heard you," and keep talking about their swimming pool!

At that point, I told them in an aggravated tone, "I hate to be this way but, I do not give a damn about your swimming pool. I gave a phone number to call." And, I hung up.

The behavior of the pool customers was shocking to me. People can be so self-centered and cruel. Not everyone did this, but several of them did over the next few days.

Around 4:00 p.m. That day my family started arriving from North Carolina. My mom was sick with a cold, and she was emotionally upset.

My brothers were being my strength as always. I felt some better with them here, but I had a giant black hole right in the center of my heart, and it hurt so much there is no explanation of it unless a person has the experience themselves. The pain I felt in my heart was a crushing, pain that hurt.

I had lost my father in 1999. My daddy was my idol. I adored him. I did not get to speak to him before he died and it left me extremely upset.

When mother told me that the doctors said I should come to North Carolina because the next heart attack would be my father's last, I took leave of absence from my job and traveled to be with them.

I arrived in North Carolina about 10:00 p.m. I called Mother to get directions from her house to the hospital. Mother said she was with Daddy in the coronary unit, and the staff was getting ready to transport him back to oncology. Daddy told Mom to tell me that he felt tired and that *he would see me in the morning.*

When mom got home about midnight, we both decided this would be the last night he stayed alone. She and I would take turns sitting with him. Daddy died at 4:00 a.m. February 6, 1999 before I ever got to see him. I can still remember the hurt I felt because I never got to speak to him. I wanted to tell him goodbye and how much I loved him.

I told my mother on the day Daddy died that he would build us the most beautiful house in Heaven. I could see him in my mind working to build us a beautiful home to live in when we meet him in Heaven. I knew in my heart Daddy was building that house for some reason.

I have a close spiritual friend in Florida by the name of Irma. Irma is three quarter Cherokee Indian. She has long gray hair, and she is average in size. She is also an ordained minister, and we have been friends since 1988.

Irma told me after Daddy died that he left me a message. She said, "He said he would *see you in the morning* and morning comes much quicker than you think."

I lived for several years remembering those wise words from my dear close friend.

Later in the day, I had to choose a funeral home and write the obituary for my son. This was also hard, but it had to be done. Mom helped me with the obituary, and we were crying and talking about the night before Kris died. She was being so kind and tender with me.

I looked at her and said, "You know Mom, Daddy must be almost done with the house in Heaven, and he needed a painter."

She said, "May be."

And then I said, "Or maybe, God took Kris because he would have had such a hard time losing me, I was all he had in the world, you know."

From the moment, I found my son dead I started trying to figure out why God had let him die. I did not know why but I knew this I did not want to be here on earth anymore without my precious son, Kris.

There is something about having to write your child's obituary that is just not right. This should not happen. A parent should never have to write a child's obituary. It sounds so final…it is final.

We got the obituary written that evening, and I had a sick feeling inside that it was all true. I went to my room and cried for the rest of the night. I could not eat, and I could not sleep. I could only cry and hurt.

I would like to say that I do understand when parents experience the job of writing the obituary for their child. It is a horrible thing to have to do for any of us. Sadly there is much more to come.

I dedicate the following poem to my father
Glen R. Hogan. August 5, 1935 – February 6, 1999

MY DADDY

My daddy was just a carpenter
A plain old country man
He was good, and he was honest
His word was the shake of his hand

He taught us to love one another
To remember we are all the same
No one was better than we were
For your mistakes to take the blame

My daddy loved us unconditionally
Tanned our hide from time to time
But if we ever truly needed him
He stood next to our side

He taught us truth gave us justice
And family gave us pride
To keep God in your heart
And your loved ones by your side

He taught us to keep an eye
On every single man
Because not everyone
Had been taught to understand

Yes, daddy was just a carpenter…
Wise in so many ways
He taught us that we were accountable
For everything that we do and say

He taught us life made no promises
To bring us a glorious pass
To work hard and be honest
That was all that he would ask

My daddy was just a carpenter
I miss him every day
But the lessons that he taught me
Will forever inside me stay

I love you, daddy.

~Renee Hogan Blythe

CHAPTER 3
THE FOG

● ●

For the next several weeks, I lived in a *fog*. It was like everything was in slow motion and nothing was happening for real. It seemed I was dreaming it all. There was an endless list of things that had to be taken care of, and many things had to be taken care of by me.

I had a long conversation with the doctor who did the autopsy on my son. I was on the phone with LifeNet Health for what seemed like hours. Being a donor was a decision that Kris made for himself. He had the donor heart on his driver's license. I remember thinking to myself, "That's my Kris always thinking about others."

LifeNet Heath promised me that I could have an open casket without anyone being able to tell he had given his eyes, bones and tissue. They kept their promise.

I could hear some conversations going on about what happened to Kris. Many people speculated that Kris had used drugs to cause his death because of his age and his use of drugs at one time in his life. Personally, I knew in my heart that he was not on drugs.

It was almost three months before I got the autopsy results on the death of my son. The doctor determined that his heart stopped in his sleep. He was disease free, with no drugs involved. The autopsy read *Natural Causes*.

Can anyone please tell me, what is *natural* about dying at age thirty? A close friend said, "Imagine having SIDS at age thirty."

Several times during Kris's life he said he wanted to be buried in a pine box. He would say, "Mom if I ever die I want a pine box like the cowboys had. Just dig a hole, no vault or anything and bury me. I want to go back to dust."

I would laugh and say, "Well first of all you are not going to die before me and I would look cute putting you in a pine box if you did."

After Kris's death, I ask Patty if he had ever discussed his wishes with her, and she answered, "Yes, he wants a pine box."

I found out quickly that pine boxes are not available, and a vault is mandatory by law. I found myself in disbelief that I was even discussing this subject of the *pine box*.

When Mom and I were at the funeral home making arrangements and discussing the pine box, I noticed a wooden box on the cremation shelf. So I decided to purchase a casket and have a viewing and service and then have my precious son cremated and put in a pine box. Today, he is in his *pine box* here at home with me.

Making a decision of cremation was a hard one. After I think about it, I think Kris would say I am not here anyway, and since he said he wanted to go back to dust, I have learned to live with my decision of cremation.

Another reason I chose cremation is because I am from Arkansas and I was not sure I would stay in Virginia. I could not imagine leaving him buried here and not being close enough to visit. So my decision may be self-centered in some ways. However, because of this decision, I am choosing to be cremated myself.

For the next few days, people came out of the woodwork.

I saw people I had not seen in years. I had people coming in that I had never met who knew my son. I had neighbors and neighborhood taverns bringing in food.

One sweet lady came in with champagne and a generous bowl of fruit, and she said to me, "I am Mrs. Phelps and your son painted my house. He painted the outside first and did such a good job I hired him to paint the inside. He was such a delightful young man, and I did not want him to leave because I had just had hernia surgery and he pampered me, so I hired him to paint some furniture."

She said, "This may seem inappropriate, the champagne and fruit, but he was just so bubbly and he loved his mother so much. He told me many things about his fantastic Mom."

I cried some more. She said, "I helped Kris paint the furniture because he said he had not painted furniture before and I have paint under my fingernail. I hope it never goes away." She touched my heart in a kind way that day.

Kris had been painting for several years, and I received dozens of emails from people I did not know. They all told me how much he talked about me and the love he had for me. It felt good, and it felt awful all at the same time.

The funeral was on Friday, June 6, 2008 at 3:00 p.m. I would not let them close the casket. For some reason, I refused to see my son closed up in a casket. It stayed open for the entire service.

Kris looked asleep and unusually peaceful. Many people came to the funeral. His best friend, Jason did the eulogy and my best friend Janet wrote a poem in his honor and read it at the funeral. *This poem will be at the end of this chapter.*

We had a collage of pictures of Kris and some lovely music. Three people got up and spoke about the short time they knew him as their painter and what a terrific person he was. It touched my heart to know that people would take time out of their day to go to their painter's funeral.

When the service was over I asked for some time alone with

Kris, and I explained to him that he would be coming home with me. I did not plan to throw his ashes to the four winds or bury him in the ground. I told Kris that would come later when they laid me to rest.

I walked out of the funeral home that day never to see my precious baby again. I think that was the most difficult point in my life.

It seems to find him dead that early morning should be the most difficult time in my life, however, walking out of the funeral home and leaving Kris behind that day, was harder on me in many ways.

We had a celebration of life at my house and several people came after the funeral. We ate and talked about all the funny things Kris would do and how much he loved to play tricks on people. Everyone signed a sturdy wall board in the garage one of his and Greg's favorite hangouts.

We talked about good times and hurtful times and had a few drinks, some things that I knew he would want us to do. He loved his weekend drinks.

I began feeling a bit of anger during this celebration. Angry because I should not be doing this, celebrating the death of my only child! I was a mess already and had not had time to realize it.

The following day, my mom and Phil had to leave, and on Sunday my brothers and their families had to leave so they could get back to work and continue on with their lives.

The funeral was sad for my brother's younger children because they loved Kris. It was difficult for them to understand him leaving us for no reason.

He was around them for a couple of years when he stayed with my mom and dad, and they had grown close. So my brother and his wife took some time to have a day at the beach with the children on Saturday before they left for North Carolina.

For me, that Saturday was a needed break. Sunday came,

and the rest of the family left. On Monday morning, I woke up all alone. It was over. Everybody had gone. However, the *fog* was still there.

I had to pinch myself to realize it was all true. But it was true. My baby was dead. He was gone forever. I cried for several hours. I felt like I never wanted to get up out of the bed again.

This fog lasted for a month or more. A few days after the service, the funeral home brought me the ashes and the death certificate. I remember thinking how heavy they were as I placed them aside for the moment.

My brother Tim had called and said he was coming back to stay with me for a few more days. Tim had a job starting in Kentucky in a week, and he and his girlfriend came to stay with me before he needed to report to the new project.

Then on Saturday, June 14th I started having trouble breathing and I fainted. Tim and Jenita helped to get me stabilized, but the breathing was difficult. It took a fan blowing in my face for me to breathe.

At about 6:00 a.m., I called Janet to come and take me to the hospital. Once they examined me, the doctor told me my lung had collapsed from the rib injury. I spent the next twelve days in the hospital.

I went through three surgeries, and because I was uninsured I received extremely poor treatment from everyone at the hospital except the chaplain. This was an ordeal in itself.

While grieving the loss of my only child, I felt some compassion was in order from the doctors and hospital staff. But no such luck. The *anger* thickened.

When I got home, Patty stayed a couple of nights with me, but she just could not handle being here without Kris around and went to her father's house.

Patty has become estranged from me since the death of Kris. I think in some ways she held me responsible for his death, and she blamed herself for not being here the night he died. We have spoken a few times in the past year, and she has moved on with her life, but she and I will never be close again.

She made a point of telling me the last time we spoke that my son did not think that I loved him. Sound familiar? I felt the same way.

The relationship I have with Patty now saddens me because my son loved her so much. And I loved her too.

By now, it was July, and the pool calls were coming in by the droves as clients were getting ready for the summer. Frank was working seven days a week and taking all of the phone calls and running the business alone. He was trying to give me some time to heal from surgery and grieve the loss of my son.

I was no help to Frank at all because every time I left my house I felt the world closing in on me. It was a strange and eerie time in my life I will never forget.

After a couple of months, I did go to work with Frank, and I became sick to my stomach and fainted just from sitting in the sun. My health was not right by any means for many months.

This was so different, especially for me because I have always been so outgoing and people friendly. Not being able to leave the house without having this *closed in* feeling was terrible. I felt everyone was watching me and I wanted to get away from them as fast as possible.

For Frank, I will always be thankful. He had lost his brother at age fifteen, and he understood my loss. I will have to say he was my supporting arm during the most difficult time of my life for five long years.

Days turned into months.

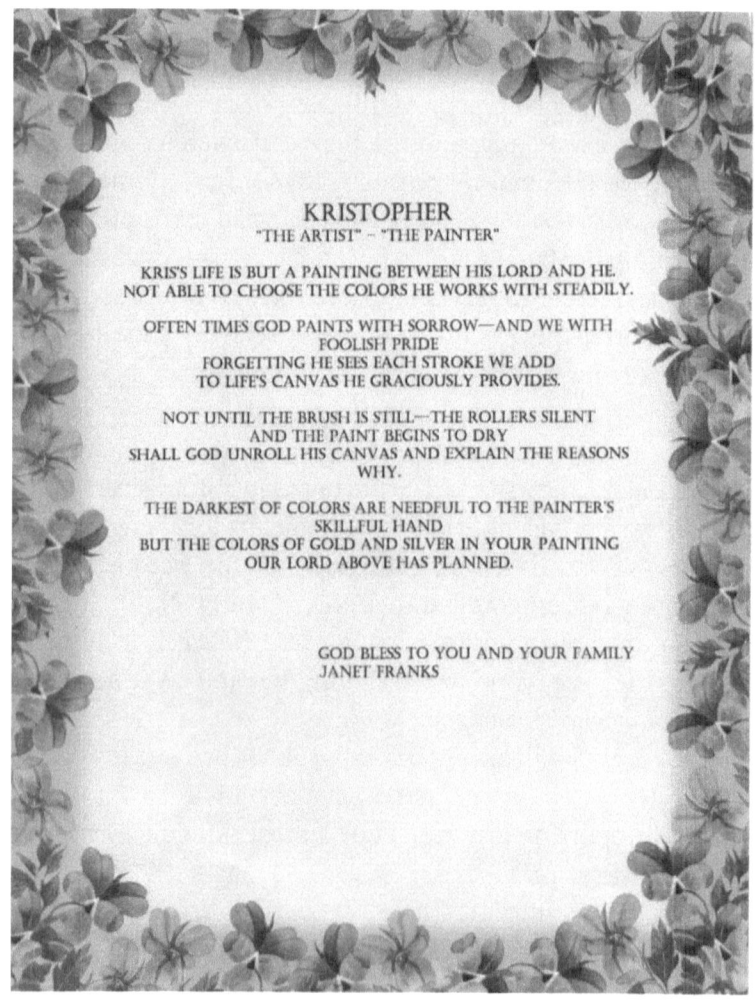

KRISTOPHER
"THE ARTIST" – "THE PAINTER"

KRIS'S LIFE IS BUT A PAINTING BETWEEN HIS LORD AND HE.
NOT ABLE TO CHOOSE THE COLORS HE WORKS WITH STEADILY.

OFTEN TIMES GOD PAINTS WITH SORROW—AND WE WITH
FOOLISH PRIDE
FORGETTING HE SEES EACH STROKE WE ADD
TO LIFE'S CANVAS HE GRACIOUSLY PROVIDES.

NOT UNTIL THE BRUSH IS STILL—THE ROLLERS SILENT
AND THE PAINT BEGINS TO DRY
SHALL GOD UNROLL HIS CANVAS AND EXPLAIN THE REASONS
WHY.

THE DARKEST OF COLORS ARE NEEDFUL TO THE PAINTER'S
SKILLFUL HAND
BUT THE COLORS OF GOLD AND SILVER IN YOUR PAINTING
OUR LORD ABOVE HAS PLANNED.

GOD BLESS TO YOU AND YOUR FAMILY
JANET FRANKS

THE PAINTER

CHAPTER 4
FEELING ALONE

I had several visitors when I was in the hospital. Friends came in and out with flowers and Irma, my delightful friend from Florida came to see me. She has been with me on three different occasions after a surgery and cared for me during recovery.

This lady has helped both me and my son find Jesus Christ, Lord and Savior. She was with Kris the day he baptized at Rock Church in 1997.

Mom and Phil made another trip from North Carolina to visit me in the hospital, but I had to stay a week longer than expected, so they had to leave before I went home.

When I came home, I had Patty for a few days. By then my brother and his girlfriend had left for the job in Kentucky. Life for everyone had gone back to normal. I started feeling extremely alone. I started re-living finding Kris dead over and over day after day. It was heart wrenching.

I started keeping a journal and wrote to Kris often. I especially like writing to him first thing in the mornings, on his birthday and holidays. I just told him what had been going on and how much I loved him. Sometimes I caught myself just going on and on about things that had been happening in the pool business and at home. It gave me a sense of closeness for some reason.

Some people make memory books or scrapbooks. Some plant a tree or buy a star. Some people make a quilt from their children's clothes. Parents look for anything they can find to help keep the memory of their dead child alive.

I have a shelf in my living room that Kris built for me when he was in high school. It now holds my son's ashes in his pine box and many of his personal things along with a guardian angel. There are also pictures of my Daddy, Robert, my grandmothers, my uncle who have passed and the latest addition a picture of Winston, Frank's brother. I call it my *memory shelf.*

LifeNet Health has been a blessing in so many ways. They stayed in contact with me and sent me many invitations to events they arrange for donor families. They sent me a lovely memory book to fill out and keep. They also introduced me to the support website where I could vent and express my feelings.

The Mormon girls were my only visitors for about the first five months after the death of my son. I talked to mother on the telephone almost every day, but these two young girls were my only visitors. I was in shock that all of my friends just stopped calling or coming over to see me. I had an extremely hard time understanding why. Losing my friends, hurt almost as much as losing my son. The loneliness was overbearing.

The hospital bills started coming in by the dozen. The funeral home bills started coming, and the collection calls started next. My sad, lonely life became a total mess.

My whole life had turned upside down in just one quick moment on June 3, 2008, and I felt so empty inside with nobody to turn to for help. Kris had always been there when I needed help and he had left me.

I spent many days and nights dealing with PTSD and loneliness. I cried and begged God to let me die. I got angry because I woke up in the morning. I was in total misery. I thought of Kris constantly. After all, I had spent thirty years thinking about him every day. That has never changed, and I do not think it ever will.

What has changed is my perspective on life in the world we live in today. I have many different opinions from those I had five years ago. I have done much research and read hundreds of books looking for answers. I have begged and pleaded with God for answers. I have thought about suicide and I have thought about living again.

The long road of grief has no right or wrong way and I believe that everyone grieves in their own way. Some people can just accept it, and others cannot. Some pretend it is not real while others re-live the moment over and over. Some people cannot cry, and some cannot stop crying. I told a close friend just today. I have cried a river and gained a whole person and begged to die. However, I am still here for some reason.

Letting myself get in the shape I am in today is my fault. However, I can finally say I am willing to try to live again. It has been a long journey and took a lot of hard work but one day at a time I have reached a good place. I feel that it can happen for others if it can happen for me.

One of my dear friends who lost her daughter over seventeen years ago at the age of 18 in a car crash said to me, "Renee, I lost Kimberly, and I still have a terrible time with this loss, but I can at least say I still have Lisa. I cannot even imagine losing your only child at age thirty."

I appreciated Liz saying that because I did not only lose my only child. I lost my family. I will never be able to bear another child. I will never be a grandmother. There will never be an extension of me in existence on this earth. I lost my life when I lost my son. Starting over has not been easy.

Just last year, another dear friend, lost his three year old son to MRSA. My friend, Christopher knew my son Kris, and he and I have become close since the death of his three year old, Christian.

Christopher is Doris Ann's step son. I have known him since he was fifteen years old. He owns a limousine service here in the Hampton Roads area of Virginia.

I try to help Chris get over some of the hurdles I have experienced already during grief and suggest some reading material. He and his wife have another baby now. Meagen is their beautiful baby girl who is healthy and growing.

Christopher's grief is keeping him distant from Meagan, the new child because of fear that his son, Christian will see him playing with her and get upset because he can no longer be here. This just goes to show how grieving parents not only imagine everything in the world, but they live it. All of the feelings like these are normal.

One thing during all of the loneliness I experienced was *guilt*. There is a whole chapter on guilt later in my book, but the first sign of guilt was the first time I laughed. My son was dead! I had no reason to be happy! How dare *I* to laugh and have fun? It was a strong feeling I lived with for over two years.

Loneliness is overwhelming. I feel lonely at Christmas. I feel alone on Mother's Day, which is still one of the hardest days for me. I feel alone on Kris's heaven date. I feel alone on my birthday. I feel alone most all of the time because so many people around me do not understand how losing your only child affects a person.

Personally, I have a problem understanding why my life and all the work I have done for over thirty years has been a waste and for nothing.

Little did I know that feeling *lonely* is not even half of this long journey they call grief.

DO NOT CRY FOR ME DADDY

Do not cry for me Daddy
I am right here
Although you cannot see me,
I can see your tears

I visit you often
I go to work with you each day
When it is time for you to close your eyes
On your pillow is where I lay

I hold your hand and stroke your hair
And whisper words in your ear
If you are sad today Daddy
Remember, I am here

God took me home
This we all know is true
You will always be My Daddy
Even though I am not with you

We will never be apart
For every time you think of me
Please know I am in your Heart

~Author Unknown

CHAPTER 5
POST TRAUMATIC STRESS DISORDER

•••••••••••••••••••••••••••••••••••

Post-traumatic stress disorder is an anxiety disorder. It can occur after a person sees or experiences a traumatic event that involves the threat of injury or death.

For years, I had known veterans with post traumatic stress disorder, better known as PTSD, and I had a good understanding of it. Some of my veteran friends went through government programs offered to them for PTSD. I became pen pals with some, and tried to encourage them when they were in the hospital and facing some of the struggles with PTSD created from the Vietnam War. I never dreamed in all my days that I would be a victim of PTSD.

For over four years, I re-lived finding my son dead on the living room couch that hot summer morning. There was no stopping it. It just happened over and over, mostly when I was alone. I had flashback episodes, where the event seemed to be happening again and again right before my eyes.

I also experienced emotional *numbing* or feeling as though I did not care about anything. I felt detached, and I had a lack of interest in normal activities. I avoided places, people, or anything that reminded me of that morning. I felt that I had no future.

I had difficulty concentrating. I startled easily. I had headaches. I was irritable and had outbursts of anger and I most certainly had trouble falling or staying asleep. I experienced dizziness and had several episodes of fainting for the first year. These are all common symptoms of PTSD.

The flashbacks started with me coming from the bathroom and walking toward Kris on the couch, and every second until Frank verified what I already knew that my baby was dead.

For me, denial was an enormous part of my PTSD. I was in denial of my son's death and refused to let anything change as far as home and Kris's room. I kept his room the same way it was the day he died, and I kept the couch. There was no way I was getting rid of that couch because that is where he died.

I had given a few of his things away to the family, but I kept most everything the same for over four years. I slept with the pillow that was under his head when he died for two years. I would not wash the blanket that covered him for four years. I refused to let anyone touch anything that belonged to my son. I was in total denial that he was not coming back and did not realize it.

Finally, in 2012 I got rid of the couch and bought some new furniture. Frank and I made some improvements to the house, and I went through most everything in it, and I made some decisions about the things that belonged to Kris.

Letting go and giving up the battle inside me, helped me to make some dramatic changes, which in return helped with the PTSD lived daily.

Since I have removed the couch from my home, I have had only two distressing dreams so far. The day terrors have ended. I pray they never come back.

I chose not to seek professional help for PTSD although I knew I needed it. I refused to look for help. I felt I was strong enough to persevere through this long nightmare all by myself.

If I had taken the time to see a professional and listen to

someone other than me, I could have saved myself years of struggle. For this reason, I am including this chapter. It is for stubborn parents like me who try to conquer it all on their own.

Parents who are re-living the death of a child over and over with symptoms of PTSD should look for professional help. Understanding that PTSD it is normal during the grief process may prevent some from believing they are losing their mind.

I know there are steps to be taken to lessen the pain. Try to let go and change the scene first and foremost. Avoid the place where your nightmare began. This can only help. It is what helped me. By all means, please seek professional help.

The PTSD may never end entirely for me, but at least I have taken the first step in making an effort to help this situation. I know in my heart I am better today because of it.

God bless parents who are experiencing PTSD. I do understand these reoccurring nightmares. Yes, it is normal.

I AM HERE

I can see you sad and in so much pain

I shed some tears that you call rain

As I watch you cry and hear you scream

I try to comfort you with a dream

As I walk beside you every day

You cannot see me, but I'm there anyway

I see everything that you do

I am always very close to you

I am the bird in the tree

See that butterfly...It is me

I am the breeze; the fallen snow

I am the light of the sun; Don't you know?

Please do not cry mommy dear

I love you more, and I am here

~Renee Hogan Blythe

CHAPTER 6
THE GUILT

• •

I am positive there is not one living parent who has lost a child from death, and not experienced the feeling of guilt. Even if, we are guilty of nothing, it is human nature to blame ourselves.

After all, we are the parents! Parents are the ones who are responsible for protecting their children and keeping them safe from harm. Parents are the ones who make sure the children eat properly so they will not get sick.

I have a list of *if only* a mile long. If I had only asked Kris if he felt crummy the night he died, I maybe could have helped him. If only I had walked over to him when he was sleeping at 3:00 a.m.; Maybe, I could have saved him. If only I had said "I love you", instead of saying, "thank you son for cooking dinner."

If only I had been a better mom. If only I had insisted Kris go to the doctor more often. If only I had paid more attention to him. The list of *if only* could fill my book.

I have felt guilty about every foul word I had with my son. We loved each other very much, but we had a fair share of arguments over things I did not approve of him doing, or things he did not approve of me doing. When people ask me about Kris, I make a point to tell them to be careful what they say to their kids. I go on to explain that if anything ever happens people remember every foul word spoken to their child whether it was intentional or not. I have spent many nights on my knees praying for forgiveness because of things I said to my precious son that I did not mean.

Guilt like sadness overwhelmed me. The guilt caused the anger to rise in me and caused me to blame myself for all of it.

I now believe we have no choice when it is your time to go back home. This is out of your control. If death *were* under your control, every single one of your children would still be alive today, all of them.

Even though, guilt is a part of the grief process, it is not necessary. Parents feeling guilt should acknowledge your guilt and then read the eighth paragraph of Chapter 6 in my book over and over. We unquestionably have no control over anyone's death, not even our own.

I spent hours feeling guilty about not doing more things with Kris and going more places with him when he became older. I would cry because I should have taken him on more vacations and planned one day every week just for him. I thought of every little thing that should have been different so the short time he had here on this earth would have been better.

Think about these things when experiencing guilt. So what if you did hand them the car keys? Ask yourself this. What if you had not handed them the car keys? Would he or she have driven the car anyway? Most likely they would have.

What if you were out of town when it happened? Ask yourself, if you had been in town would it have changed what happened? The answer is, probably *not*.

What if another child is living a healthy life and they had the same cancer as your dead baby. Are you going to blame yourself and feel guilty because they did not have the same doctor or the same hospital?

And what if they did have the same disease and the same

doctor and same hospital? Are you going to feel guilty because you should have done more? Disease affects every person differently because we all have a different DNA. We have no control.

There are hundreds upon hundreds of ways and reasons to feel guilty because your child is dead. I have experienced most of them. Guilt is a dead end road my friend. Guilt will not change anything but your personality, and your attitude toward life in the long run.

I finally realized that the love I have for Kris is just as strong now as the day he died, and the day he took his first breath. There is no reason to feel guilty because God knows that there is positively nothing, including giving my own life that I would not do for the life of my son.

I hope parents can take some comfort in knowing the same thing in your heart. There is much more than guilt to deal with, and people can do a whole lot better without it. I can finally say my feelings of guilt have gone.

Earlier I mentioned the guilt I felt when I laughed or caught myself enjoying something. I have spoken with several parents who experience this same feeling of guilt.

After about two years of feeling guilty when I laughed, Doris finally convinced me to visit her out in the country for a day. She and I were talking about some of the fun things we would do together, and I caught myself laughing and here came that guilty feeling again.

I talked to Doris about it, and I discussed the feelings I had been experiencing with her. I also read a book on guilt and did a lot of praying. Now I find laughter to be some of my best medicine.

Laughter creates a substance in the body that keeps us well. It is true. My prescription for guilt: One good belly laugh per day.

Some medical knowledge I will share is from three different doctors who treated me while I was in the hospital right after

Kris died. It takes the human body approximately eight months to function normally after the death of a child. There have been hundreds of studies done on the grief process and how the body responds to treatment during grief of a close member of the family.

I had a fractured rib when Kris died, and it had been over six days since it happened. The doctors explained that the body makes a fluid to cushion the heart and lungs when there is a chest injury. In most cases, the body will absorb the fluid as it heals.

They believe what happened to me had a lot to do with the death of my son. They explained that because I was so emotional and upset the body started making more and more of this fluid. The extra fluid collapsed my lung. They removed five liters of fluid from my chest cavity.

My healing process was slower than other surgeries I had recovered from in the past. I understood why, and I believe the doctors are correct about the eight months. It took at least eight months for my body to start feeling normal again. The rest of my misery was self inflicted because I stopped caring about me. Now I have to deal with those consequences all by myself. I am currently working on getting myself back to normal.

Guilt is something hard to get rid of altogether. I have even felt guilty for feeling better. The difference now is I can realize the feeling of guilt for what it is. Today, I can acknowledge the guilt and then put it aside because I know in my heart that my love for Kris has not changed for even one minute since his birth and it never will.

Guilt is not from God, so it has no place in my life anymore.

GUILT

Will I stop feeling this guilt someday?

The guilt I feel since my child died that way

Maybe I should have been aware

Could the life of my son be spared?

Why did I not do more for him?

Maybe things would not be so grim

What did I do with all of my time?

My child is dead now

Things will never be fine

God, please, please tell me why

This guilt is eating my insides alive

I know that there must be the reason

Please help me to understand

I would give my own life or cut off my hand

God, please take me to Heaven instead

Things will never be the same

With my baby dead

~Renee Hogan Blythe

CHAPTER 7
MY VISIT

●●●●●●●●●●●●●●●●●●●●●●●●●●●●●●●●●●

Before I discuss my visit, I would like to say that I understand not everyone may believe as I do. I choose to believe that our loved ones are still around us.

I often wonder how many parents have similar experiences and choose not to share because someone might laugh at them, or say they are crazy.

Personally, I believe there are quite a few parents who have unusual experiences and wonder if it is just their imagination.

After my return home from the hospital, I was alone in the house and sitting in my living room on *the couch* crying and praying. I said the Lord's Prayer at least twenty times a day for years.

Kris came to me that day, and we talked. I did not visually see him, but he talked to me in my mind and answered all of my questions. Yes, I too, thought I was just imagining it. So I tested him.

He said, "Mom do not cry I am okay."

I said out loud, "It is not Kris. I am just imagining all of this."

"No mom, I am here, right here with you!" Kris spoke in my mind.

I said, "Okay then, why did you die?"

Kris said, "I just went to sleep."

And, then I asked him, "Did you have a choice to stay or go?"

He answered in a sad tone, "Yes."

I screamed, "Why did you leave me?"

He got all excited and said, "Mom! It is so beautiful here! There is no pain, no sorrow, and no hate. You will understand someday."

I asked Kris, "Is Daddy there?"

He answered enthusiastically, "Yes, Pa is here, Mamaw is here, Betty is here, Jay is here, Granny is here, my dad is here and Mamie is here."

I said, "How did you get so lucky to leave this earth?"

Kris replied, "I straightened up. You will understand someday Mom."

I told Kris, "Go right now and tell God I want to leave here to be with you and Him in Heaven. I do not want to be here on earth any longer."

Kris sounded sad when he said, "It's not your time Mom you will understand it all someday."

And then, he says in a real excited tone, "Mom did you see how many people were at my funeral?"

I knew that very instant it was him talking to me. I would have never thought that about his funeral.

The funny part is Kris did not know Mamie; she was my babysitter when I was a little girl. From there, we just talked and spent the day together. Kris hung out in the kitchen with me while I cooked and let me know in his own unique way he was there with me, and he was okay.

Later, I went out to the garage and told Greg about the experience I had with Kris. While I was chatting with Greg and sitting in an office chair we had in the garage, it kept tilting back over and over. Greg was watching this! Greg said, "Yep, that is Kris! You know how he loves to aggravate you." I have not had another visit like this since that day.

I just want parents to know that if some do have an experience or a visit or some communication from your dead child or loved one, you are not crazy. It is normal.

I had a visit from my grandmother when she died back in 1997, as well. My father was in the hospital with leukemia and his mother died in Arkansas. My mother and brother Tony went to Arkansas to make funeral arrangements for grandma while I went to stay with Daddy in North Carolina.

On the drive to North Carolina, my grandmother talked to me all the way there. She said, "Now Hon, do not worry about Mamaw, I understand that you will not be at my funeral. I want you to take care of Glen (my dad). He needs you with him right now. Glen is crying because he cannot be there for me and he does not need to feel that way because I am not here anymore."

She said once again, "I am fine and in a beautiful place now."

Then she started talking and reminiscing about me when I was a little girl and would stay with her. She would laugh and tell me stories and tell me how much she loved me. She stayed with me until I got to the hospital to be with Daddy.

On the way home, Mamaw came back and talked to me on the drive home and told me that she was one of my guardian angels. She said that I could call for her if I ever needed her for anything. That was the end of the visit and the last time she spoke to me.

Now that, I am thinking of it, I visited a medium about one year after Kris died and she did not have any communication with Kris, but she did say that two of my grandmothers and a Native American Indian were my guides or what some people call guardian angels.

I think loved ones are much closer than we think. I have no proof. I only have my experiences.

After Kris's death, I had a part-time job and a man had stopped to chat with me about a product I was selling which led me to the question, "Are you a doctor?" He said, "No, I am a spiritualist."

I said, "Oh yeah, my son died about six months ago can you talk to him?" Next, he gave me a reading.

He said, "Yes, he is here and he says to tell you that he loves you."

"I know that he loves me!" I exclaimed, and rolled my eyes.

Then the spiritualist says, "He is saying to take care of his cat."

Now he is laughing out loud and saying, "*big and brassy!*"

He is saying "Tell my Mom not to move, to rent my room or something, but not to move because something very good is going to happen to her."

Next, he told me that Kris had left.

This reading set me back on my heels. I did not think he would be able to pick up on my son in the first place, especially in the middle of K-Mart, but I believe he did. The strangest part is Kris did have a cat named Charlie Chan, and he loved that cat. Charlie is Siamese and something else. Kris knew I was not a cat person.

I was selling fake jewelry, and I know that was the *big and brassy* comment because I had been selling real jewelry before he died.

I had also been contemplating a move to North Carolina, as well. My mother encouraged me to wait awhile before I made any decisions about moving.

I am still waiting for the good thing to happen, mentioned by Kris in that reading. I believe the time on the other side is much different from time here on earth. So in other words, something good can still happen. I think I will just continue to wait.

Only a few days after Kris died, a lady told me about her daughter dying from cancer at the age of twenty eight. She has a son, but she expressed how much she missed her daughter. She told me about a year after her daughter died that God gave her a beautiful dream one night. She said it was so real as if they were together one more time and she found immense comfort from the dream.

She promised me that God would give me a dream someday. I have waited and prayed and prayed for my dream, and I have never had one, not even one. This tells me that God works in different ways for each one of us. He knows your needs better than we do. He knows your heart better than we do.

He is an all loving God and we are *all* His children. I know how God felt when Jesus died on the cross more than I ever thought possible today. God is on your side.

Before I close this chapter, let me say that my mom gave me some darned good advice. She told me to wait at least one year before I made a decision about moving because people think more rationally after a year.

I had an urge to run away after Kris died. I wanted to run from everything so that his death would not be so real. After about a year, my thinking changed about running away and moving. I have never moved even though I considered moving early in my journey of grief.

WHEN WE DIE

When we die
We get new wings
And all of Heaven's Angels sing
We get a chance to talk to God
He answers questions
Even the ones that seem odd
We find that life had a reason
For every living thing, there is a season
A time to come home where we belong
A time to rejoice and sing Heaven's song
We have no pain
We have no fear
Heaven is beautiful
Every day of the year
We get permission to watch over the ones we love
To help them from up above
We are not dead and lost forever
We are sitting by your side
Until we are back together

~Renee Hogan Blythe

CHAPTER 8
FRIENDS AND COMMENTS

● ●

I touched briefly on friends in Chapter 4, but I want to take some time to tell other parents about what happened to me. I want to do this because I have spoken over the years to many people who have lost a spouse or child and found themselves in the same situation. I cannot help but believe that several people experience a significant loss of friends.

For about one year before Kris died I had been working on swimming pools. It was not the cushy sales positions I had grown accustomed too, believe me. The pool business is a dirty job. It also limited my association with people. Since we ran the business from home, there was no office to go to, or employees to hang out with, so falling into a space where I could stay home happened easier for me than for most people with a job outside of the home.

After my return home from the hospital, I found myself alone most every day. The phone had stopped ringing the visits had stopped and then I noticed even my friends did not stop by anymore. I did call my friends to say hello to them.

They would say I have been busy and just have not had time to come visit. I will stop by in the next week or so. That week or so has never come for many of them, and it has been over five years.

After about five months, Sandy, one friend of mine who faithfully came to see me every week for years stopped by for a visit.

Sandy is a feisty young woman in her late thirties, with brown hair and brown eyes. She is a single mom of two and works hard to support her children. We became friends in 1996 when she started working at the same company I worked at for over fifteen years.

The day she came to visit, I had a long talk with her about why she had stayed away for so long. She cried and said she did not know what to say, and she wanted to give me some time.

I told her that I needed her now more than ever before, and there was nothing she could say to make things better. The only thing that would make things better was for Kris to come back and that was not going to happen. I explained, losing my son is distressing enough but losing my friends too has only made things worse.

After the visit Sandy came over as always, but she was the only one for almost three years. It saddens me extremely to think that the so many good friends I thought I had, simply could not think of anything to say to me.

I feel some better today about how my friends treated me after the death of my son. I think the real truth is they could not stand to see me sad. They had a life, and they felt sorry that I had lost my son, but being around a sad person is not good for them or their family. It is almost like we have a contagious disease and they are afraid they will catch it from us.

The smile I can manage to put back on my face today attracts new friends. So I know the sadness because of the death of my son has got to be the true answer. My friends could not stand seeing me different and different I am.

I know if I have heard it, other parents will hear it from someone; *They say only the good die young.*

You're so blessed that he died peacefully.

Well honey, at least he did not suffer.

Feel fortunate that he did not get killed by someone or hit by a drunk driver.

Remember that God gave You Kris for thirty long years.

You will see him again someday.

He is right here with you, this very minute.

The things people said to me should have been comforting but they were not.

I believe even when people have the best intentions and just try to let parents know that they do care, the parent who has a dead child *knows* there is no way they can understand.

Many of the statements I just made are true. My son did die peacefully. I am lucky that Kris did not get murdered by someone, or killed by a drunk driver. We did have thirty beautiful years together, but the *words* just do not help.

One of the most devastating things said to me was by Shelia (not her real name). Shelia lived next door to Kris and me for about eight years and had moved a couple of years before Kris died.

One day, about six months after Kris had died, I took someone home that needed a ride, and when I dropped them off Shelia was in the parking lot and motioned me to stop. So I did, thinking she just wanted to give her condolences, and she said, "I heard about Kris, and that mother fucker deserved to die. I'm glad I do not ever have to look at his sorry ass again."

I wanted to run over her with my truck. I was extremely angry. Instead, I looked at her and laughed at her and said, "Shelia there is nothing that anyone can say to me that will hurt me more than I have already been hurt. You will *never* have to worry about seeing Kris again because people like you will not get to Heaven." I drove away.

People who are intentionally cruel to parents after they suffer the loss of a child will surely experience the hurt themselves someday. I believe in Karma. *What goes around comes around!*

Talking to people who had experienced the loss of a child did help me. At least I knew they knew how it felt. You would not believe the stories I could tell about the mean things people say after someone loses a child. It is incredible.

I was told that it is time to *get over it*. One person said I enjoyed wallowing in grief because I went to the *Grieving Mothers* support group on *Face book*. I was told that I am on a pity party, and people did not like me because I cried.

I can promise this, I have never enjoyed one minute of this grief journey, and I will never just *get over it*.

Other parents who had lost a child helped to guide me through some of the grief process and made the journey a bit easier. I believe each parent has to walk the road we're given in their own way.

Your journey of grief is another one of life's lessons, and I can say I am a better person today because of it. I have spent a lot of time reading my Bible and talking to God. Time I was too busy to give before.

I have changed my attitude about so many things in life, as well. Material things do not mean anything to me anymore. I am happy with what I have. After all, I no longer have anybody to leave my belongings too.

I am much more spiritual than I was, and I believe differently than I believed before. I feel certain that I will go to Heaven now, and I am certain I will be with my son again someday in a much better place than we live in here on earth.

Even as I write about my journey it has not ended. I will continue to grow spiritually and earn my righteous place in Heaven.

Just today, I snapped at a dear friend out of the stress I am feeling sharing my journey of grief with other parents, and I had to call to apologize to him. He had no idea my state of mind or what I had been doing, and it was unfair of me to be so short with him.

So I am still climbing the hill one day at a time, but there is a light now. The darkness is finally lifting.

THINKING OF YOU

I think of you before I sleep

I think of you when I wake

I know that you are in Heaven's gate

My heart cries out for your touch

I miss you son so darned much

If I could have one more minute or two

There is nothing I would not say or do

My baby is dead that is all I think

Gone suddenly in one quick blink

If only I could turn back time

You would still be here by my side

I know this will never be

Please, please do not forget me

I will be coming to see you soon

Keep waiting son

Keep waiting for me

Next to you is where I want to be

Love, Mom

~Renee Hogan Blythe

CHAPTER 9
THE SHUTDOWN

●●●●●●●●●●●●●●●●●●●●●●●●●●●●●●●●

Death affects everyone in a different way. Some people can accept death as a part of life. Up until the death of my son, I could follow those feelings. Death is a part of life.

When my father died, I thought it was the worst thing that had ever happened to me. Daddy had leukemia, and we (the family) knew he would not be with us long. Even knowing our loved one is dying, we are never ready for someone that we love to leave us.

I did not get the chance to say my final good-bye to my father, and that bothered me for several years. However, I was able to maintain my job and go on with everyday life. I missed Daddy terribly and caught myself wanting to talk to him so many times.

On June 3, 2008, my only child died. This time was different. I did not accept his death as just a part of life. After the funeral, my ordeal at the hospital and the loss of close friends, I went into total *shutdown*.

I experienced days and days of not wanting to get out of bed again. I prayed to die each and every day for over three years. I did get out of bed and try to live eventually but my world as I had known it was in total shutdown.

I just simply stopped caring about everything. I did not

want to clean house. I did not want to go to the grocery or even outdoors. I did not want to get dressed or put on makeup or cook. I did not want to do much of anything but cry and die.

After about five months, I ventured out and worked for awhile, but the minute I came in from work I went back to bed.

I believe that parent's experience shutdown more frequently than those who lose a parent or sibling. I believe some people also have the *shutdown* experience when they lose a spouse, and they have no children. As I keep mentioning, everyone grieves in their own way.

For parents experiencing shutdown, know this is normal. It is not normal to do it, but it is normal to experience it.

I will tell parents from my experience shutdown is another epic waste of valuable time because it will not change anything. For the three years, I went through this period of my grief journey it only triggered more problems with my health, weight and general well-being. Kris is still dead. It did not change that fact.

Shutdown is a syndrome to me. It feels as if someone has put your body in a deep hole and nobody or nothing can pull you out. It was during this shutdown part of my grief journey that I considered suicide on several occasions. So it is not a good place to be.

Since I have shared my consideration of suicide, let me say that suicide was a silly thing for me to think of doing.

I have always been a particularly outgoing person who loved people and being out and about in the world. This shutdown I experienced was way out of context for me, and it was just as hard for me to walk through and find the end. I felt my world was taken away and for no good reason that I could find.

It is also during this time that I started searching ways to start healing. I read my Bible and about anything I could find on losing a child. I read spiritual books. I went to LifeNet

Health's family site and started talking to other parents who had lost a child.

I talked to Liz and Irma and other people that I could find that had experienced losing their child. I found out quickly there are millions of us.

Personally, I chose not to go to group meetings, but others encouraged me to go many times. I am sure these special groups have helped many people.

There are self help books available for grieving parents. At the end of my book, readers will a find a list of books that I feel brought me some comfort.

For parents that have other living children, I beg them to focus on the surviving children. They have lost a sibling, and they, too need a parent. That focus could help stop your experience of these grueling shutdown years.

I think if there is a purgatory the shutdown experience can be compared. It feels as though we are wallowing in misery. This is the only comparison I can think about today.

I am so glad it is finally over.

THE HOLE

I woke one morning, and my child was dead
Nothing can ever be the same
I do not want to go on living
I will never hear him say my name

I am in a hole
I cannot get out
It is cold in here
Can God hear me shout?

My life is over
It is not worth living
I feel so empty inside
And Satan ridden

How can it be?
My life has changed
I cannot be me
I am not the same

Help me God
To find a way
To leave this place
And have a smile today

~Renee Hogan Blythe

CHAPTER 10
THE CRYING

●●●●●●●●●●●●●●●●●●●●●●●●●●●●●●●●●●●

After crying a river, I am an expert on the topic of crying. I absolutely had no idea I had so many tears in my body. I cried every day for four long years, and I still cry today.

I am finding that I do not cry as often, and I have many days in a row that I do not cry at all. However, last night I caught myself crying and talking to my baby.

Parents may be interested in knowing that I have felt guilt for feeling better and *not* crying before. It is true!

When Kris died I had to deal with change and a host of feelings including shock, anger, guilt, fear and sadness. Crying was acceptable at first. I expected to cry and understood crying for the first several months. It was after years of the crying episodes that I started doubting this journey would get easier for me, or the crying would stop.

I can remember waking up crying every morning for over three long years because I simply woke up. I had prayed to die! What was wrong with God? Did He hear my prayers? The crying lasted for the first hour in the morning until finally I could get a grip and get busy in the office for the pool company.

If I found myself with any free time, here came the tears. I cannot even count the times Frank walked in the door and found me crying. He simply got used to finding me this way and said nothing except occasionally he would say, "You have got to get a grip, and try to do better."

I began to question my sanity. What is wrong with me? Are things ever going to get any better? Is this the life a grieving parent will always lead? It led me to think my only way out of hell was self-destruction.

Crying is a very real part of the grieving process that I have dealt with. I believe some people cannot cry because they put up a psychological wall and refuse to live the grief. They often find themselves year's later dealing with tears and going through the crying process. I believe it is because we all grieve differently.

After three, years, I started to become more conscious of my crying and started hiding it from people. I would not let anyone see me cry, I did that alone. The crying did not stop, however.

Only about a year ago I visited a local tavern for an afternoon drink and some socializing and a song came on the jukebox, a song Kris and I both loved, Bohemian Rhapsody by Queen. The tears hit me as I was talking with a girlfriend I had to get up and go into the restroom. As the tears gushed from my eyes, another friend came from behind a closed door in the restroom to comfort me, and I had to apologize to her.

It had been almost four years since my son's death, and I felt ashamed. She said she understood, but I did not understand. I knew only one thing, and that was in some way the crying had to stop when I was around people.

In January of 2012, when I made some changes and put Kris's personal belongings away and changed his room my crying started to ease some. I caught myself going a day or two without crying.

Eventually, I caught myself talking about Kris without crying. Each day, the crying, crushing heart pain and sleepless nights seemed to be getting better. I have cried several times writing about my journey and remembering all I have been through, but I can say I am better today.

I ran into all kinds of things that would cause me to start crying. It could be a song on the radio, a baby or small child that reminded me of Kris, even a scent of his favorite food or cologne that could have an effect on me.

Crying is normal. Wondering if something is wrong with your feelings is normal. Asking if things will ever change is normal. The fact of the matter is that when we have lost a child we never *get over* the event, we simply learn to live with it.

For me, I believe death and tragedy are not feeling torn and unrepaired, but more a matter of learning to incorporate the experience into the person we are going to become.

I am now someone who has experienced a tragedy.

The loss of a child is an adaptation, not a recovery. We're not *broken* we're *changed*. A parent must find room in his or her character and personality to incorporate this change into your life.

I cannot promise that the crying will ever fully stop, but I can promise that crying for many years is normal.

Renee Hogan Blythe

LULLABIES

Daddy, please do not look sad.
Mommy, please don't cry.
I am in the arms of Jesus,
and He sings me lullabies.
Please do not try to question God.
Don't think He is unkind.
Don't think He sent me to you, and then
He changed His mind.
You see I am special.
He needs me up above.
I am the special child you gave Him,
the product of your love.
I will always be there with you.
Watch the twinkling sky at night.
Find the brightest star.
That is my halo's brilliant light.
Daddy, please do not look sad.
Mommy, please don't cry.
I am in the arms of Jesus,
And He sings me lullabies.

~Author Unknown

CHAPTER 11
THE ANGER

My first hint of anger was at the celebration of life we had for Kris after his funeral. I felt so angry that I was celebrating the death of my son. I knew in my heart I was doing what Kris would wish me to do, but celebrating!

I was angry because this should be someone else … not me. Little did I know it was only the beginning of the anger I would experience. I believe the anger stage can creep in just about anywhere during the journey of grief but at some point parents will have anger.

The next time I felt anger was in the hospital when the nursing staff and doctors were so cold over the death of my only child. I felt they could give some compassion for my feelings.

The anger thickened when my friends stopped calling me and coming by to visit. I was so lonely, and I needed them so much.

It was almost two years before I felt anger toward Kris, but I did. I was mad as hell because he left me. He promised me that he always would be here and that he would take care of me someday. Kris did not keep his promise. He left me.

I was mad at Kris because he would not visit me as he did that one Saturday afternoon a few weeks after he died.

I was angry with him because he would not visit me in

my dreams. It had to be *his* fault. I caught myself turning his pictures over so I could not see them. How childish!

I was in a place that I stayed stuck in for so long, and the anger kept building and building.

I mentioned earlier that I never blamed God or got angry at Him because of my son's death, but I did get mad at God because He was not listening to my pleas for His help!

During this anger stage, I was short spoken to everyone. I think now about the poor customers who called for pool service and had to hear this bitter voice over the telephone must have felt. Sometimes I would catch myself and just stop and tell them, "I'm sorry, but my son died about two years ago and I am experiencing a bad day."

Usually they understood, but it still did not make what I was doing right. There is an old saying that goes...*Hind sight has 20/20 vision.* That one saying applies so well to me today. I can now look back and see so many things that could have saved me from wallowing in self-pity. That is why I am writing about my journey, to help just one person possibly avoid some of the pain I have endured.

There are hundreds of parents who are angry at doctors and hospitals because they did not save their precious child. There are others who are angry at the people responsible for the death of their child.

Some parents are angry at the emergency services. Some are angry at their spouse because they should have done something to prevent what happened.

I believe that we look for any reason we can find to make sense of this terrible loss, and to understand the reasons why. I think we get to the point in the grief process when we are not getting the answers we need, so we get *angry.*

Anger can be placed anywhere during this process. Many feel anger right away. Many parents feel anger toward God. Some parents are angry at themselves. Some are simply mad at the world, but it will not change the circumstances. Anger will not bring your baby home.

This journey of grief is heart-wrenching in every way. I think if we just try to get the information we need to help us cope with the feelings we feel, we might be able to get through the process a little easier. It has taken me a long time to accumulate this knowledge, and I might add that even though I chose to read many books to help me along, very few of them brought me total comfort.

This reminds me of what I said to my doctor when I was in the hospital. He offered to give me a prescription for anxiety because of the death of my son. I said to him, "No, I do not need a bunch of drugs. I have to walk through this pain I feel, and drugs will just *cover up* what has happened to me. When I stop taking the pills given to me, I will still have to live through the pain anyway so I might as well start the journey now."

That was a wise decision on my part. My friend, Christopher lost his child a little over a year ago, and the doctors have Christopher on five or six prescriptions. He does not know himself anymore. This makes me sad because I know in my heart Christopher's journey has not ever begun.

This reminded me of something else I wanted to share.

I have heard mentioned that the mother feels more grief than the father because she is the one who carried the child inside her by the cord. Let me say, I do not believe this is always the case. There are many fathers who mourn the loss of their child. In many cases, they have a more difficult time with the loss than the mother.

Christopher is a perfect example. There is no right or wrong way to grieve. One person does not feel more pain than the other one. We just all deal with what we feel in a different way. So before, we go to sleep tonight, just take one minute to say:

Our Father who art in heaven,
Hallowed be thy name
Thy kingdom come

Thy will be done
In earth, as it is in heaven
Give us this day our daily bread
And forgive us our trespasses,
As we forgive those who trespass against us.
Lead us, not into temptation, but deliver us from evil:
For Thine is the kingdom, and the power,
and the glory, forever and ever. Amen.

This prayer has gotten me to where I am today. It has helped me to stay in touch with God. I can pray a different prayer today and ask God for the things I need in life again, but for a long time I could only get this one prayer out of my mouth.

At the end to the Lord's Prayer, I would say, "Heavenly Father, please give Kris a kiss and hug from me and tell him how much I love him and miss him. In Jesus name, Amen.

We all need someone or something to help us, and I believe my help came from God above.

ANGER

Why must I feel this anger?
When I am so lost and numb
Why must I feel this anger?
For the loss of my son

I want to hit somebody
I want to scream out loud
I miss him so deeply
I hurt among the crowd

Why must I feel this anger?
And feel so left alone
Why must I hate my life?
All because my son is gone

Can God hear me?
Can God hear my cries?
I want to have my baby
Again next to my side

Why must I feel this anger?
Each and every day
I need your help Heavenly Father
Please erase this anger away

~Renee Hogan Blythe

CHAPTER 12
THE CHANGE

●●●●●●●●●●●●●●●●●●●●●●●●●●●●●●●●

When your baby dies parents wake up to a changed world. Whether your accustomed to preparing baby bottles; waiting for children to arrive home from school; making a weekly visit to see a child, or waiting for a daily phone call, parents who have a child die find themselves thrust into a new world. Your life has suddenly changed forever.

After the death of my son, I would catch myself listening for Kris to open the front door and walk in the house with his paint brushes and lunch box. He always arrived home around 5:00 p.m. He would take his paint brushes in the bathroom and clean them and get ready for the following day, make himself a drink and get something to munch on until dinner.

On Friday, he would come in with a bunch of groceries and drinks for the weekend, cook and entertain. He also helped me pay the household bills.

The change that affected me the most is the *first thought* in the morning. For over thirty years, my first thought was about Kris. I need to get up and feed Kris. I need to get Kris ready for school. I need to take Kris to the dentist. I better make sure Kris is okay. Today, my first thought every morning is still about Kris. That has not changed.

I have had to come to terms with this waking moment, and I have spent the majority of the mornings with tears in my eyes. You simply wake up to a reality that your baby is dead every single day. He is not here. Starting your day with tears wears the body down and only thickens the sadness.

When a song came on the radio that Kris and I both loved I remember saying, this is mine and Kris' song, and happily sing along. After my son's death, when the same song would come on the radio, I cried. The singing had stopped.

The scent of his favorite food, something I would find in a drawer or the garage somewhere, the scent of the cologne he wore, the Discovery channel, anything that Kris loved would cause me to cry.

I caught myself looking for things he loved to eat at the grocery store. I caught myself looking at clothes I thought he would like to wear when out shopping. I caught myself in the electronics department looking at electronics Kris did not have already. I would look at things I thought he would like for Christmas or his birthday. I caught myself making plans and thinking of including him. He was gone, but my thoughts did not change about him for a long time.

I remember the disappointment I felt inside when I called his cell phone and he did not have a recorded message. If only I could hear his voice! I know I would have called his phone one hundred times a day. However, my Kris had to have a Sprint message and not his voice.

I did not make videos during my time with Kris. I do not have anything with his voice recorded. But guess what? That voice is in my memory, and I know exactly what he sounds like even today. I can hear him, and see him so clearly.

Adapting to this horrific change was exceedingly hard for me. At this time, I started developing my *new normal*.

My salvation has been Jesus Christ. Jesus has helped me in so many ways to get better today.

When I woke up this morning my first thought was about

Kris, as always, but instead of crying, I thought of Kris with Jesus and waiting for me.

I believe we all have a destiny in life, and until we live it, we stay right where we are. We can stay in grief forever, but until we realize we do have a destiny we will be here on this earth until we step out of grief long enough to fulfill that destiny. I would hate to think my only destiny was to experience the excruciating pain of grief I have felt for the past five years.

It came to a point I had to at least get up and try to find out what is my destiny. I feel part of my destiny is to share with other parents what I have experienced since I lost Kris, my son and only child.

This part of my destiny in life is challenging and difficult, but if it can help even one mom or one dad get through the journey of grief just a little easier, it was all worth it. By writing my book, I have made some type effort to fulfill my destiny whether it was God intended or not.

When we face change, we have to look for new ways of doing things. After the death of a child, we have to get up differently, cook differently, clean differently, go places differently, buy things differently, and even go to bed differently.

I have often wondered why this change has been so different from the other changes I have experienced in my life. After all, going through divorce more than once, was change. My daddy died, and that was a change. I have moved no telling how many times in my life and that was change. However, the change from the loss of Kris was not the same in any way as the others.

I believe it is because children are a part of us. You can read the poem *The Cord* at the beginning of my book to understand the meaning here.

Some of the other things I have done to help me is taking Kris with me when I travel. I have a small urn with his ashes, and he goes on trips with me. I buy him a Christmas ornament every year for the tree. I buy him a Christmas decoration every year for his birthday on December 15th. I still make him a birthday cake and send him helium balloons.

I cook his famous recipes he invented. I listen to the songs he put on his mp3 player. I buy the electronics he would get excited about for me. I write letters to him in a journal on holidays and when I get to missing him real bad. I keep his pictures around me. Whether people enjoy hearing them or not I tell funny stories about Kris.

Kris may be gone, but he does not have to die completely. I can keep him alive in my heart by remembering him and talking about him. When my book is complete, I pray a few more people will know about him.

I want people to know what an incredible person Kris was. He had such a sweet heart. He only wanted for people to like him. He was a hard worker and sharp as a tack. He was an artist, and from what his girlfriends has told me, Kris was a romantic.

Kris was caring and always willing to help someone. He loved Jesus, and he loved his mom, his family and his friends. He was my son in every way possible, and I love him dearly even though he is dead.

So if, you are going through change, which I know you are, just know in your heart, you too, can start creating a *new normal* one day at a time. God bless every parent who reads this, and may He be next to everyone every moment of every day. Amen.

Renee Hogan Blythe

CHANGE

My life has changed forever

Never to be the same

No one left to care for

No one to call my name

The name my son gave me

He always called me Mom

My life has changed forever

My heart is never calm

No, presents to buy at Christmas

No birthdays for us to sing

Just another day to remember

The day he got his wings

My Life has changed forever

I listen for the door

Each day I hear silence

Not like it was before

I miss his happy laughter

The messes he would make

I miss his cookout parties

And the drawings he made

My life has changed forever

I sing a different song

I am lonely and saddened

Everything feels so wrong

I lift my eyes to Heaven

Every day I kneel and pray

That God will help change me

In a better way

My life has changed forever

The memories will never die

I cherish every moment

I see him as I close my eyes

My life has changed forever

My son is in my heart

I am living for the minute

We will never be apart

~Renee Hogan Blythe

CHAPTER 13
THINGS THAT WE SAY

●●●●●●●●●●●●●●●●●●●●●●●●●●●●●●●●

This is a chapter in my book that I had to think about for a long time before I decided to include it. Let me say before I tell this part of my story that most people have *not* experienced this phase in their journey. After much consideration, I thought maybe someone has experienced this or something similar, especially estranged parents.

To begin, I want to talk a little about me beginning at the age of ten or eleven years old. I was the oldest child in the family and unquestionably spoiled. I had two younger brothers who aggravated me all of the time. My feisty ways caused me to say things such as *I am going to kill you,* or *I wish you were dead!*

I can remember my mom saying, "Now Renee, you should not say things you do not mean, you might get what you wish for, and you would not wish to see your brother dead."

My mom gave me a lot of good advice that I did not understand until later in life. I was staring at a lady with acne on her face one day, and I asked my mother "What is wrong with her face?"

My mother's answer, "You should not say anything about someone, you might have that someday."

Once, she caught me staring at a handicapped person at the grocery store and Mom said, "Renee, Do not stare. You would not appreciate someone staring at you if you were in a wheel chair."

Over my lifetime, I have said many, many things that I should not have said. I have said things out of anger, out of frustration, out of ignorance, even out of concern in some cases. Most of the wrongful things I have said to people have come back to haunt me.

It reminds me of scripture, "He who is without sin, let him cast the first stone." (John 8:7) Meaning throw it if you must – you who are without sin.

The absolute worst thing I have ever said in my lifetime was to my precious son when he was drunk. This was about six months before he died on my living room couch.

Kris was drunk. He annoyed me by acting drunk and poking at my arms, and I was pleading for him to please stop. He insisted to keep aggravating so I got angry, and while pushing him away from me, I said *I wish you were dead!*

The very instant those words left my mouth that day, I felt humiliation and guilt. I did apologize the following day to Kris, but I felt I should have never uttered those *hateful* words, especially to my son. Six months later he was dead.

At this time, readers can go back to my Guilt Chapter and add this one! I know Kris knew I did not mean what I said. He had me angry. However, somehow, someway, I know I should have never, ever defied my mother's teaching. God has forgiven me, and today I ask my mother to forgive me too.

Here is the rest of the story. Because of the condemnation of myself, I became extremely bitter. Do you feel sorry for me? Feel sorry for Frank. He has been the person to endure my self-loathing.

I have shared this story with close friends and family and explained the difficulty of my guilt. And I continue to hear the same two answers, "He knows you did not mean it" and, "You know you should not have said that." Today, I believe both are true.

Not too long ago, my brother sent me an email that was pretty straight forward. He said that I was on a pity-party, and his family did not want to be around me and watch me cry. He also reminded me that I wished my son dead. At first I was terribly angry and swore I would never speak to my brother again. Today I would like to thank my brother Tony for telling me the truth and helping me to take a good, long and hard look at myself.

I also want to apologize to Tony, his wife Janet and his family for any harsh things I have said to them. I have been insane for five years. *Please forgive me.*

Things that I have said extend to my friends and others who barely know me. When I think about myself over the past four years, I think about an old scrooge or a miserable being. I have been bitter because people could carry on with their happy lives and I could not.

I have gotten mad because the majority of my friends and my brothers have grandchildren and I do not nor will I ever have a grandchild.

I have been mad because friends interrupted my self-loathing. I have told people not to come over to my house. I have refused many invitations.

If my car broke down, I did not care. If I did not cook dinner, I did not care. If the bills did not get paid, I simply did not care. My life became an extremely unhealthy place, even for me.

I want to say, *Thank You* to all of my friends for trying to be my friend. I am sorry for being harsh today. I know now that my friends were trying to care about me. It is hard to care about someone when they do not care for themselves.

Grief is hard enough to deal with without saying things we do not mean to other people. I know it is hard to stay sane when all your thoughts are about your dead child and things that should be different.

The truth is this. No matter what we do, we have a forgiving

Heavenly Father, and when we ask Him, He forgives us. There is not one thing anyone can change about the past. Let it be said. Let it be done.

Now, I will *close* this chapter in my life.

AN UGLY PAIR OF SHOES

I am wearing a pair of shoes.

They are ugly shoes….uncomfortable Shoes

I hate my shoes.

Each day I wear them, and each day I wish I had another pair.

Some days my shoes hurt so much that I do not think I can take another step.

However, I continue to wear them.

I get funny looks wearing these shoes.

The looks of sympathy.

I can tell in the eyes of others that they are glad they are not wearing my shoes.

They never talk about my shoes.

To learn how awful my shoes feel might make them uncomfortable.

To understand these shoes, a parent must walk in them.

But, once you put them on, you can never take them off.

I now realize that I am not the only one who wears these ugly shoes.

There are many pairs in this world.

Some women ache daily as they try and walk in them.

Some have learned how to walk in them, so they do not hurt quite as much.

Some have worn the shoes for so long that days will go by

before they think about how much they hurt.

No woman deserves to wear these shoes.

Yet because of the shoes, I wear, I am a stronger woman.

These shoes have given me the strength to face anything.

These shoes have made me whom I am.

I will forever walk in the ugly shoes of a woman who has lost a child.

Author Unknown

I dedicate this poem to my brother Tony and his family with love.

CHAPTER 14
DEPRESSION

●●●●●●●●●●●●●●●●●●●●●●●●●●●●●●●●●

Depression is a part of grief. I believe we all experience some depression. I have.

There have been other episodes of depression in my life. I experienced depression for over one year after a failed marriage. I was a step-mom for seven years. I left behind two children that I grew to love dearly, and that was hard. I often wonder if it had not been for Kris how I would have gotten through that terrible state of depression I lived in at the time.

I have always been a happy person with a great love for people. I have always been interested in learning about them and things they do. I enjoy telling jokes and laughing. I love to entertain and have guests. I love to dance. So much of me has changed from the *old me*.

Depression has been extremely difficult, and I still have some depression but no longer the deep depression I felt for almost four years. Deep depression (or clinical depression they call it) is the place we are in when we start thinking about self-destruction or stay in bed and never want to get up.

I know I spent one full year sitting in a recliner in my living room crying every single day. I tried to stop crying when someone was around, but the times I spent alone were the worst. When sadness, loneliness, and depression get wrapped up together, you discover you have quite a mess on your hands my friend. It is hard to figure out which one to work on first.

Most people I would speak with about my depression suggested that I see a doctor or go to group counseling for grief. After my bankruptcy, I refused to go back to the doctor for any reason and groups of the grieving was not a place I wanted to be, so I dealt with my depression in my own way.

One friend told me about his experience with depression and how it got him down and how he wanted to stay away from people all of the time. He said getting back out and around people helped him to come out of his depression. I tried getting out more. It did not help.

I read several books on depression. I got a better understanding of what depression is, but the books did not help. I caught myself looking in the mirror and seeing the change in my appearance, and I would get even more depressed.

I think my recovery from depression started about the time I accepted my son was dead and was never coming home. I had made some changes at home including changing Kris's bedroom, and I got rid of the couch. I started taking interest in how things looked at home. I found myself staying busy doing things other than sitting around crying. I painted my dining room furniture, re-painted the trim in my house, cleaned the paneling in my room and cleaned the oven. I spent a good three months just going through everything in my house, re-arranging things and deep cleaning. I began to feel better.

Last summer, Frank's mother told me that she started taking some art classes to help her depression after the death of her youngest son. She explained by doing things she enjoyed such as painting and planting her flowers she found some inner peace.

Sometimes I think we just have to take care of ourselves. I know it can be hard when all of your thoughts are about your dead baby, but unless we make some effort nothing ever changes.

Depression may be described as feeling sad, blue, unhappy, miserable, or down in the dumps. Most of us feel this way at one time or another for short periods. True clinical depression is a mood disorder in which feelings of sadness, loss, anger, or frustration interfere with everyday life for weeks or longer.

Doctors recommend anti-depressants or talk therapy. Personally, I think medication for depression after the loss of a child is not a good idea. Covering feeling slows down the grief process. I believe we must walk through it, to get through it, and there is simply no other choice. We do it now, or we can do it later.

I can honestly say this today my depression comes more from what I have done to myself than the loss of Kris. I have walked through the depression from losing Kris, but the mirror does not lie. I have gained weight my eyes look sad, the corners of my mouth look sad. I have aged.

The past five years have taken a toll on me. I have started working on me, and I am losing some weight, but I often wonder if I will look in the mirror and see me again. If I do not, at least I can say I have tried.

I have found getting more exercise, maintaining good sleep habits, seeking activities that bring me pleasure, talking about my feelings and trying to be around people who are caring and positive have helped my depression.

I go to joke groups on the Internet at least two or three times a day and read jokes that make me laugh. I join the *Pajama Party* on Grieving Mothers on occasion where we wear pajamas, *do not cry,* and laughter is plentiful for an hour or so. We meet tell jokes and act silly.

Positive breed's positive, I have always believed that. Even though, depression has been a huge part of my life for the past few years, I know staying positive can only help.

For today, take some time to smell the roses. Take some

time doing something just for yourself. Smile even though it hurts and your, not in a mood to smile. Things will slowly get better. We must crawl before we can walk.

DEPRESSED

I'm sitting in my lonely room

Feeling life's given gloom

I cannot get up to comb my hair

I feel my life is total despair

How can I go on living this way?

The same old feelings every day

My heart is sad...

My spirit has broken

How can I go on with no hope spoken?

Show me a light from Heaven above

Send me your lasting and fulfilling love

I need you God, more than ever before

Please rescue me and open a door

~Renee Hogan Blythe

CHAPTER 15
THE SADNESS

●●●●●●●●●●●●●●●●●●●●●●●●●●●●●●●●●●●

For me, the overwhelming sadness I felt was even worse than the loneliness. I was so sad inside it was crushing. I felt something had a hold of my heart and had just ripped out a part of it. I have said many times half of me died with Kris.

In the middle of November 2008, I took a job doing jewelry shows at K-Mart. It got me out of the house and helped me to get back around people. I had suffered with the *closed in* feeling I mentioned earlier in my book for nearly three months. I had to be able to go out to buy groceries and do some things to keep the household running. I felt a job might help me. It did help me too.

I made some decent money working every day, and suddenly found myself in the midst of the holiday season around busy shoppers. December is a hard time of the year for me. Kris's birthday is on December 15th and then my first Christmas without him was right around the corner.

On the first Christmas without Kris, I will have to say that my family and Frank's family went all out to make me feel comfortable during the holidays. I gave each person in my family a gift from Kris, just a little something that belonged to him. However, the sadness was so intense, I just could not enjoy Christmas as hard as I tried.

I was so glad when it was all over, and I could go back home. Since then, I have learned Christmas is no longer for me but the children. I try to do something unique each Christmas for some child in need.

Even though, I have never been angry at God over my son dying, I have felt many times his death is punishment for my mistakes. I do not think we ever know until someday when we take the journey to heaven and find out. I know God has my baby, and I am doing my best to be good so I can be with him again. I pray to God every day and ask Him to give Kris a kiss for me and tell him that I love him. After what Patty said to me, I can only hope Kris knows how much I love him.

Those words *Kris did not think that you loved him* that Patty spoke to me hit home in more ways than one that day. I did not know he felt that I did not love him. I knew we had disagreements, but I loved Kris will all of my heart. I mean all of it. The thought of Kris thinking that I did not love him makes me tremendously sad inside.

For me, anger with God is not the answer. Some people feel a lot of anger toward God because they have told me so. However, from all I have read and from what I have lived through, I think that anger subsides when we gain control of the senses enough to realize that God loves us.

In many ways, God protected me by giving my son a peaceful death at home. I know people who were not that lucky. My spiritual mother, Irma found her twenty four year old son dead in the attic. He committed suicide. This happens every day to parents and my heart breaks for them.

Sadness took me looking for things and people to blame for my son's death. It caused me to stop caring about things that were important to me at one time.

I stopped caring about me more than anything. I stopped going to the nail salon, I gained weight, I stopped visiting my friends, stopped wearing a bra, stopped getting dressed until the afternoon. I just sat at home and cried day after day after day for over four years.

At one point in my grief, I blamed my sadness on the hundred thousand dollar hospital bills, the bill collectors calling daily, Frank, my family, my friends, anything I could find.

I decided to start working on the problems. I filed bankruptcy to get rid of the debt and lawsuits and collections calls and got that behind me.

A few friends started coming by to visit again, but the sadness never left me. I worked the following summer in the pool business running the cleaning crew. The sadness stayed struck to my heart like glue. I would say to God, "Please help me!" I am so *sad* all of the time.

Last year, Mom and I talked, and I told her that I thought the sadness was the hardest part of all of this grieving process. I tried to explain to her how defeated I felt all of the time because the sadness would not go away or leave my heart. Sadness can swallow us up if we let it and I did.

It has been five years since the death of my son, and some of the sadness will always be with me. A few months ago God finally said I had to get up and do something or nothing would ever change for me.

Since I listened to Him and started making an effort of some kind, the sadness is still there but not as intense as it has been in the past. I feel better and I have started taking better care of me. After all, *Me* is all I have now.

Parents who are finding sadness overwhelming, I would like to say it is normal. It is sad, but it is true.

Do yourself a favor and do not let sadness totally overwhelm your heart as it did mine. It is one of the most difficult things to overcome. I am still trying.

SADNESS

My mind is tatter

My heart is sore

All I can feel is a constant mourn

The sadness is deep

It will not go away

It engulfs my being every single day

I miss my son

I want him home

I will never make it through this alone

My heart cries out for his hug and his touch

A smile from his face

I miss him so much

Why did my God take my baby from me?

And break my heart for eternity

~Renee Hogan Blythe

CHAPTER 16
APPETITE & ANXIETY

● ●

APPETITE

Many people report physical symptoms that accompany grief. Stomach pain, loss of appetite, intestinal upsets, sleep disturbances and loss of energy are all common symptoms of acute grief. Of all life, 's stresses, mourning can seriously test your natural defense systems. Existing illnesses may worsen, or new conditions may develop.

When your heart is in your throat, it can make it hard to eat. For the first few days after the death of my son, I could not eat. I did not want to eat. I think most of us feel this way.

Afterwards, in about my third month of grief I started eating to feel comfort and in the past four years have gained almost one hundred pounds.

Eating provides us the nutrition we need to function properly. The body is going through a transition due to the shock and emotional stress associated with the loss of a child so providing nutrition is essential. However, over eating to find comfort leaves a person with more heath problems and a large challenge to get the weight off. A challenge I personally could do without after everything I have been through for the past five years from the death of my son.

I can look back now and see my mistakes. If I had spent

time walking and crying instead of eating and crying, I would look pretty good!

Be good to your body is my advice. Do not get fat looking for comfort or get sick from not eating properly. Someday, we must face the health issues that we create.

I have started eating small meals especially in the morning, and I keep some vegetables around to snack on or some fruit. I have a small lunch and a nutritious dinner so I can sleep better. I try to think before I eat now. For those who are not eating, think before you don't eat!

I understand it can be hard either way, but with everything else we are dealing with your health is something a grieving parent should do their best to keep in control. I am living, waddling proof.

I promise we *will* want to live again someday.

ANXIETY
For parents, the death of a child elicits severe anxiety and other negative emotions associated with loss.

Social anxiety disorder, also called social phobia, is an anxiety disorder in which a person has an excessive and unreasonable fear of social situations. Anxiety (intense nervousness), and/or self-consciousness, can arise from the fear of someone watching, judging, or criticizing.

Social anxiety is what I experienced for the first three months after the death of my son. I think I referred to it earlier in my book as the *closed in* feeling. I could not stand being in public or outdoors. It took me *making* myself get out and back around the living to get rid of this terrible feeling.

I have read that personal death anxiety is a condition that afflicts many women who lose a child. Whether a parent loses a child during pregnancy, as an infant or toddler, or later in years, the development of personal death anxiety is the same. As a grieving parent, you may notice a sudden awareness of your own mortality and a sense of anxiety over the potential loss of your own life. Physicians recommend treatment for this form of anxiety.

I had many anxiety episodes where I felt I was drowning in my own thoughts, crazy thoughts that came to me by the thousands. I could not stop them. I felt that my life was literally coming unglued. I felt that I was experiencing a nervous breakdown. I could not shut down my thoughts.

I became obsessed with thinking about what happened to Kris. I thought about every minute from the time he walked in the door from work until the minute I found him dead on the living room couch. At times, I felt that I could not breathe.

I believe anxiety manifests in many different ways. You may feel you are smothering and have breathing attacks. A person may feel as if they are on a merry-go-round and cannot get off. They may have so many thoughts at once they cannot determine which one is real. Anxiety plays tricks on us and forces us to believe things that are not real. Just knowing what anxiety is can help.

Parents that are experiencing anxiety should know it is a normal part of the grieving process. If a grieving parent feels a physician can help, by all means see one and get some medication to help the panic attacks. Try not to take medication for too long, however.

We must walk through grief without covering up the pain to get through it and find peace. The Lord's Prayer is one of the best resources I have found.

SHATTERED

Humpty Dumpty sat on the wall

Humpty Dumpty had a great fall

It was a Spring Day in June

Early one day before noon

My heart shattered then

Never to be put together again

My son lies there dead

And as I said, my world went tumbling down

As I sit here today, thinking of Humpty this way

I can understand what they said

When all the Kings horses and all the Kings men

Could never put Humpty together again

My life will never be the same

I barely hear my son's name

As Humpty Dumpty, I have fallen apart

And I have a hole in the center of my heart

~Renee Hogan Blythe

CHAPTER 17
THE BLAME

• •

For some reason, blame is a part of the grieving process that is normal. Single parents may experience a different blame, but, unfortunately, many married parents find some type spousal blame in most cases.

Personally, I did not have a husband at the time of my son's death in 2008. Kris's father died in November of 2007, just a few shorts months before Kris left me and went to be with Jesus.

I did have Frank, my companion and business partner; however, I am positive if Frank had not experienced a terrible loss himself years before, we would not be together today.

The experts say parents typically never *get over* the loss of a child, but learn to adjust and to integrate the loss into their lives. Still, the death of a child remains one of the most stressful life events imaginable.

One-fourth to one-third of parents who lose a child report that their marriage suffers strains that sometimes prove irreparable.

I believe that when we are experiencing guilt and can finally accept there was nothing we could do to prevent the death of the child, we start to *blame*. We have a need to place fault somewhere.

I read an article that says the following. The first six months following the loss of a child are when the majority of divorces occur.

I read that one in five families experiences the pain of miscarriage. Some of the problems parents may experience after the loss of a child before birth or at any age include

Lack of communication

Arguments on parenting the other children

Being over-protective of surviving children

Fear of having another child

Differences about, how the other grieves

Guilt and blame

Drug and alcohol abuse

Difficulty talking about their child who died

Disagreements about the child's belongings

Deciding to get counseling to save their marriage

Problems with finances

Problems talking to each other

Shutting the other spouse out

Feeling anger and resentment

Feeling sad when the other spouse does not

Difficulty learning to live a new normal

My son died in his sleep. I am truly fortunate for this because he died at home, and I seriously had nobody to blame. However, I did try to blame Frank for it. I even went as far as asking him if he did something to Kris. I knew for a fact he did not, but I still had a need to blame someone or something.

It took over three months to get the results of the autopsy. I had no answers. My mind was running rampant during the wait. Sometimes, I think about the parents who have lost their child in a shooting, or an accident and know in my heart this must me a hard thing to endure.

I think if blaming someone would make a difference and bring children back it might be useful to us. We all know that blame will not change that.

I think the people who are responsible for a child's death will deal with legal repercussions. After fines, jail and everything else they may experience, I am more than sure they will endure a lifetime of guilt and blame of their very own.

I know the Bible teaches us forgiveness.

I found prayer helped me when I was waiting on the autopsy and trying to place blame. Today I know what my Heavenly Father has done for me, and without Him I would be in a real dark place in my life. I thank Him and praise Him daily for taking some time to help me mend. I know He will do the same thing for other parents.

I still feel my son died way too young at age thirty. I do know in my heart that Kris is in a *good place* now.

Kris is in Heaven now where I wish to be. In some ways, I find comfort in knowing he will be right there next to God urging Him to let me in Heaven. I know I have someone on my side when it is time to make my journey home.

BLAME

Why do you blame God Above?

He gives us his Almighty love

I know you miss me and place some blame

But blaming God is such a shame

He is my Father in Heaven now

He gives us strength to carry on somehow

He loves you, as much as He loves me

He gives us life for eternity

He hears when we call His name

And He forgives when we place the blame

Please do not be sad and scream at God

When we look at Him, we are so Awed

God let me send this poem to you

So that, you know my life is not through

I am in Heaven waiting for the day

You can join me at Heaven's gate

So when we try to place some blame

Please do not use the Father's name

~Renee Hogan Blythe

CHAPTER 18
FEAR

• •

I believe fear is from the devil. It is not a part of God's plan for us. To get more control of your life, the devil enjoys taunting us with fear. The loss of a child can easily stir up fear in many areas of your life.

Personally, the fear I felt was the fear of losing myself forever. I feared that I would never be the vivacious, smiling, happy woman I once was ever again. I believe half of *me* died with Kris.

After four years and six months of grueling grief I found myself begging for God's mercy. I prayed for some peace and help to get some of *me* back. I also read several books on the subject of fear.

Now, I can say the fear is lifting. I may never be 100% whom I was again, but a lot of the things about *me* are slowly coming back. I can laugh again without feeling guilty. I can go out and be around people without the closed in feeling. I can talk about Kris without crying. I can wake up without wanting to die. I have begun to care about my looks and my weight. I can finally say I am ready to start living my *new normal*.

I recently spoke to Liz, my friend who lost her daughter in a car accident nineteen years ago. Liz, her nickname, or Sarah is Doris Ann's sister. She is a beautician and funny as can be! She has a head full of red hair and a beautiful smile. She has dealt with weight problems just as I have and lived over nineteen years of grief from the loss of her daughter.

Liz started telling me the fear she has dealt with in her journey. She said that every time Lisa, her living daughter was late coming home after the death of Kimberly she would sit in fear that Lisa was in an accident. She said she would start calling all of her friends looking for her until she found her.

She also told me one of her biggest fears was the fear of losing her marriage. Mike did not grieve in the same way as Liz. He was more subdued and quiet. Liz had trouble believing Mike or Lisa hurt as much as she did. She said she had a long journey of fear and still to this day experiences the feelings of fear for Lisa's life and Mike's life.

I have also read many articles on fear. After the death of a child or family member, fear affects almost everyone who has encountered death due to anything other than natural causes. People fear the house burning again, another drive by shooting, another dreadful car wreck, water because of a drowning, and they even fear getting out of bed in the morning. I still have fear of finding Frank or Greg dead as I did Kris.

Here, a few scriptures about fear that can help give some encouragement. These are the words from the Heavenly Father.

Deuteronomy 31:6

Be strong and courageous. Do not be afraid or terrified because of them, for the LORD your God goes with you; he will never leave you nor forsake you."

Isaiah 41:10

So do not fear, for I am with you; do not be dismayed, for I am your God. I will strengthen you and help you; I will uphold you with my righteous right hand.

Isaiah 41:13

For I am the LORD, your God, who takes hold of your right hand and says to you, Do not fear; I will help you.

Isaiah 54:4

"Do not be afraid; you will not suffer shame. Do not fear disgrace; you will not be humiliated. You will forget the shame of your youth and remember no more the reproach of your widowhood.

Matthew 10:28

Do not be afraid that. Rather, be afraid of the One who can destroy both soul and body in hell.

1 John 4:18

There is no fear in love. Perfect love drives out fear, because fear has to do with punishment. The one who fears is not made perfect in love.

Today, I have a perfect love for mankind and myself. I am spiritually stronger than ever before. Believe me when I say that I did not do it alone. It took many years of prayer and study to get me to a place where I can feel at peace.

Fear was a part of my transgression. Fear that I would never be the same. I know today that I will never be the same. I am not afraid that I will never be *me* again. People will learn to love the *new me* because I am a better person than I once was.

For parents who have lost a child and have other living children, I know the *fear* factor must be grand. Try to remember that when we are walking in fear, it is the devil's way of keeping us down and that God is on your side. Remember, I said you have positively no control over anyone's death, not even your own.

I suggest that parents call a family meeting to talk to your other children and to your spouse about the fear experience and why. Ask them for consideration because of your fear and ask them for more frequent communication to help stay out of fear.

You might find the other children have no idea how you are feeling and how much fear you are living. We are so lucky we have cell phones today! I think about the people who did not have the convenience of this quick communication years ago. It must have demanded some long days of sitting in fear.

I am sure the fear will never leave everyone as it has for me. Liz says her feelings of fear are much better now than they were for years. Keep praying. God is not fear. God is pure love. God is on your side. I promise.

SITTING IN FEAR

I sit in my room today full of fear

That something will happen to someone dear

My child died this year

How can I live with all this Fear?

I am afraid to leave my home too far

It scares me when my family drives a car

This fear consumes me every day

Is this fear here to stay?

I tell my children to stand close to me

So I can see they are okay

They face no harm

Just for today

I hate this feeling of constant fear

Please help me God

I pray you hear

Amen

~Renee Hogan Blythe

CHAPTER 19
SELF DESTRUCTION

Never in a million years would I have believed that me, Renee Hogan Blythe would consider self-destruction. I have always enjoyed living so much. I have always loved being with people and having a conversation. I have always tried to maintain a good positive attitude about life in general. My sales background has given me a lot of training in positive thinking. So self-destruction was never on my mind.

I can remember so vividly that on the night of June 3, 2008 thinking for the first time of self-destruction so I could be with my baby. This was the first day of his death. Out of pure habit, I snapped back and said to myself, "You cannot think this way, Kris would not want this and God would not want this." So I got through the next two years by simply praying for God to let me die every day.

In the third year of my grief, my family, Frank and some of my friends began to get irritated that I had not progressed and *gotten on with life*. I began to hear comments from them that it was time to *get over* my son's death and come back to the real world. People said they did not want to be around me because they did not want to see me cry. One friend said I needed to be locked up somewhere for real.

I had friends start to encourage me to go and get professional help because it was unhealthy to feel so depressed all of the time. In many ways, I felt abandoned because nobody understood how I felt and why.

At this time, I started thinking of killing myself. I thought about drinking bleach. I thought about trying to get a gun. I thought about taking an overdose of pills. I just wanted *a way out* of this terrible grief and the rude and uninvited comments.

I thought people would feel better with me dead. After all, what did I have to offer anyone? I found myself spiraling down into even a deeper, darker depression.

In this phase of my grief, I got angry with God. I started shouting at Him and asking Him if He could hear me begging for His help. I started asking Him why He had forsaken me after taking the only person in life that loved me. I told God that I did not want to kill myself, but I would do it if He did not do something to help me. I found myself bargaining with God.

It did not take long for me to realize that God does not make bargains. He let me wallow in my self-destruction phase without any answers. I found myself having to make the decision all by myself whether *I* chose to live or to die.

Thankfully, I chose to live. I could not do this to my mother. I thought about what would happen to my mother because of my selfishness. Once I made this decision, God finally spoke to me.

God said just a plainly as I am sitting at my computer today, *"Renee get up and do something or nothing will ever change. You must make an effort."* I heard him loud and clear. So I obeyed.

I began to search new things to do with my time and set some short-term goals for myself. I made some plans to move from Virginia Beach and start a new life somewhere. I started taking inventory of the work I needed to do on myself. People could not see much progress, but I could feel a difference. I did not want to die anymore.

Even though, I felt abandoned by God, I believe that He was with me for those few months that I contemplated taking my own life. God has a funny way of taking care of us without us knowing.

My suggestion to parents who are experiencing feelings of self-destruction is to get on your knees and pray for help. If we need too, we can get professional help.

Try to remember what your death would do to the ones left behind. Most importantly, realize that we all have a purpose and a destiny here on this earth even if we are not sure what it is today.

There is still a life to live. There are people who love us and need us. We are essential to God's plan. We are still living for a reason.

Self destruction is *not* the answer.

IN MY DARKEST HOUR

The aching pain I feel inside

Will not go away

I cannot hide

I miss my child

My best friend

An empty void I cannot mend

I have lost my friends

I have lost my pride

I have lost the joy deep inside

I hunger for another chance

To see my son

To laugh, to dance

My family has left me behind

They cannot understand my crying pain

They do not want me to speak his name

I find myself so alone

In my darkest hour

No son, no family, no happy home

Help me find my way

To release this pain inside

I can only look to God until it all subsides

~Renee Hogan Blythe

CHAPTER 20
ACCEPTANCE

● ●

I believe one of the most crucial steps in my journey of grief was when I finally accepted that Kris was not coming back. This took almost four years.

For some strange reason, in the back of my subconscious mind, I thought he would come home one day as he did when he was at my Mom's for a year or when he traveled and did construction work for a year. I said that I knew that he would not ever be back, but I did not *accept* it.

I kept his room the way he left it. I would not let anyone touch his tools. I kept his room dusted and clean. All of his clothes stayed in his chest of drawers and closet. Patty even stopped by about one year after he had died and commented the room was still just like it was.

I slept with the pillow my son's head was on when he died. I would not wash the quilt that was on him when he passed, and there was no way I would get rid of that couch! That is where my baby died! "No, it is staying here." I would say. And I might add that even though the couch looked good it was not particularly comfortable.

I can remember finding Kris's lunch box on the front porch one morning, and I got so angry because someone had used it!

I think we lose some sanity when we are going through grief. I did.

A little over a year ago just after Thanksgiving I started making some changes. I planned to stay home for the Christmas season for the first time in six or seven years, and I did.

Getting out the decorations and going through them opened up a lot of emotion because my son loved Christmas and he loved to help me decorate for the season.

I can remember being busy with work one year at Christmas, and I had not taken the time to decorate a tree.

Kris asked me one morning, "Are we going to put up a Christmas tree this year?"

I said, "We do not need a tree this year do we?"

He said," I am going to have a Christmas tree!" So he pulled out his artificial tree from the garage and some pumpkin lights out of the hall closet that I had for Halloween and decorated the Christmas tree with pumpkins. It was so funny. But Kris had his tree.

When decorating the house this past year I had to put some things away to make room for the Christmas decorations. After the season was over, I decided to go through some of Kris's belongings and pack them or give them to someone in need.

I washed the blanket and the pillow; re-arranged his room and put a new comforter on the bed; put curtains on the windows, and changed the pictures on the wall. I believe this is when I finally *accepted* that Kris would not be coming back home. I knew he would want someone to get some use from the things he left behind.

I gave some of his clothes to the guys who work for us. I let the work crew use his painting equipment to paint my house. As I mentioned before, I finally got rid of *the couch.*

I still have pictures of Kris everywhere. I have many more pictures of him out now than I had displayed before he died. I personally find comfort in seeing him. Some people do not, and that is okay.

My mother had a portrait painted for me, and it is above my fireplace. It means so much to me. Of course, his ashes are still on his special shelf. Even though, these things are still around me, I feel differently now than I did. I have come to terms with my loss, and I have begun living a *new normal*.

The difference today than a year ago is I have finally *accepted* that Kris is not coming back home. I still have lousy days, and I still cry. I received some healing when I came to terms with my loss.

There is no time limit on when it will happen, and some parents may accept their loss right from the very start. Frank's mother said it was eleven years before she came to terms with losing Winston. He was her youngest son, and she was on a cruise and did not know Winston was dead for five days.

We all experience different circumstances and loss in a different way, and we all grieve in a different way. So when you ask yourself is it normal for me feel this way, just know in your heart the answer is yes.

The grief process was not an easy one for a very, long time. People would say that the grief would get better with time, but for so many years it did not. In fact, in some ways it got worse.

I continued missing Kris more and more, with each passing day. I had cried one more gallon of tears. I woke up every morning when I did not want to wake up ever again.

Today, I can finally say things are starting to get *softer.* I truly believe acceptance has everything to do with it.

ACCEPTANCE

I must realize my son has gone

Never to see again

I must learn to love him another way

Until me meet again

I must accept he will not be home

Or walk through the door again

I must learn to laugh and sing

And try to be me again

I must accept that my son has gone

And will not be home again

I must give my trust to God

Until we are together again

I love you son.

~Renee Hogan Blythe

CHAPTER 21
THE FAMILY

●●●●●●●●●●●●●●●●●●●●●●●●●●●●●●●●●●

Unfortunately, my family died when Kris died. Kris was my only child. He had never married or become a father so I have no grandchildren and I never will have a grandchild. I am fifty six years old now so bearing another child is not possible for me.

My mother gets angry when I say, "My family died." I will go on to explain, "Mother, I wish you could understand!" I have lost *my* whole family."

She will say, "We are your family."

I know I have a family in North Carolina and lots of relatives who love me. *My* family died when my son died. There is a difference.

I believe losing your *only* child is different from losing a child with surviving children. I believe this not only because it is what happened to me, but I believe this because many parents have told me that it is different.

They will say things like *At least I have someone else to care for during the grief process and your left alone.* I hear *I do not know what I would do without my other children they keep me going.* So for parents whose only child has died. I *do* understand.

The topic of the family can go in so many different

directions. So to begin, let me talk about the immediate family, your spouse and surviving children.

First and foremost, they need parents too. Even though, some parents feel they have failed their dead child, the other children need them. They have lost a sibling! They have watched their parents cry. They have been through a funeral. They think you wish it were them dead because they wish it was them. The blame or guilt does not end with the parent.

Here is a perfect example. Frank's brother had a fatal accident back in 1981. Frank's parents left him in charge while they were away on a cruise. I have watched him go through guilt and blame for the six years I have known him, and it happened thirty one years ago. I can only imagine how much guilt he experienced in the early stages of grief.

The death of his brother almost destroyed their family according to his mother. However, they stayed strong, and today they are still a family.

Death is hard for the entire family. I think we get so wrapped up in the stages of grief that we forget about the other family members, and leave them to fight the battle of grief alone.

Think about this. I know in my heart that your heart would be just as broken if something happened to one of your surviving children or to your spouse. Take time to talk to each other as much as possible.

Extended family is another subject we should cover and one in which I have experience. I have my mom and two brothers. One brother has one married child and one grandchild. The other brother has six children and four grandchildren. I also have aunts, uncles and cousins.

My family was here within five hours after Kris died. They were here for me during the long process of the funeral and stayed by my side. Tim even returned so I would not feel so lost and alone. They will never know how much that meant to me. I needed them all for the first time in an awful long time.

My family gave me plenty of support that first Christmas

without Kris and on my first Mother's Day without him and on his Heaven date. They would call to see how I was doing and how I was feeling more frequent than before. They made a sincere effort to let me know they loved me.

Since my family lives five hours away, I did not get many visits, so the loneliness became overwhelming. I spent a lot of time telling mother how lonely I felt. The only thing she could do is cry for me.

After about three years of calling me more frequently and making notable efforts on my behalf, my family began to lose hope I could change. One of my brothers told me how sick he was of my pity-party. The other one just did not call as much.

None of my nieces and nephews called or came to see me the way they did when Kris was here. In many ways, I felt abandoned by my family. Alot of anger arose inside of me because of the feelings of abandonment. I vowed never to see them again.

Now I can look back and say that I forgive them. After all, they have no way of knowing how I feel. I pray they never have to know. I wish to thank them for the help they did give me. I am better today.

One of my friends told me today that she went to a family reunion several years after her daughter died, and when she came in a sister pulled her aside and said, "Get ready they are going to blast you."

Sarah's daughter had been dead for seventeen years. Her family decided *for her* that it was time to stop grieving and *get over it* and decided to tell her how they felt once and for all. She went on to explain how hard family reunions were for her without her daughter and no grandchildren.

There is no time limit on grief. I have heard three years; five years; eleven years; nineteen years; thirty one years and everything in between those stated years. It would be wonderful to tell parents that, in five, years, they will feel better, but I have no way of knowing that. I am sorry I cannot tell anyone how long it will take.

This makes me want to think about the parents who do not know where their child may be, a child never found. My heart aches for them. Personally, I think we never get over loss we just learn to live with it.

It is funny, but we cannot walk in someone else's shoes no matter how hard we try. My Daddy would say, "Little girl, I cannot go to hell for you, and you cannot go to hell for me. You have to be accountable for your actions. Just make sure, that you always act right."

Daddy had a way with words most anyone could understand.

I can remember when he went through six long years of fighting leukemia. I would say, "How are you feeling Daddy?"

He would say, "With my fingers." He never lost his sense of humor even during the end days.

One December day he said to me, "I probably will not be here for Christmas next year."

And I asked, "Why are you feeling bad Daddy?"

He said, "No, I feel like I always do, but the doctors can only give a fat rat so much poison and they have given me all the poison I can take. I have no quality of life left."

Daddy went on to explain, "When a man cannot walk to his mailbox and get the mail, the quality of life is over. Renee, it is the quality of your life that matters; not the quantity."

He died the following February.

Family is family. Some us have close families and some of us do not. Some of us have both parents and some of us have no parents. Each member of a family must walk in their own shoes each day. They are the ones who must be accountable for what they say and for what they do.

Don't be too harsh the way I was. Just forgive them and keep on living. After all, we have no other choice.

FAMILY

I love my little family

No matter what they say

They often seem so distant

And they live so far away

Sometimes I get angry

Sometimes I feel alone

But without my little family

I would have no one

I miss our conversations

I miss the times we laughed

I wish things were different

But we cannot change the past

The things they said was hurtful

They did not understand

Without my son beside me

My life has no plans

Yes, I love my little family

I wish things could be the same

I pray they can understand me

For I will always speak his name

The tears are fewer now

After the years have passed me by

But my heart will always feel the burden

Sometime I may even cry

I will always love my family

I have from the very start

I pray they will forgive me

And keep me in their heart

~Renee Hogan Blythe

CHAPTER 22
DONOR FAMILIES

● ●

Because, my son, Kristopher Glen Hardrick was a donor I wanted to include this chapter in my book. For parents who are now a part of my donor family and the parents who had to make the decision for their child during a time of uncertainty and crisis, I understand.

Unlike many parents, I did not have to make the donor decision. My son was thirty years old, and he had the donor heart on his driver's license. However, I did have to give my final consent.

Even though, I knew this was a service Kris chose for himself, I had to think about it. I remembered the times I needed to decide if I wanted to be a donor over the years and marked *Yes,* once; and marked *No,* the next time. I wondered if Kris had done the same.

I did not know if I wanted these people cutting up my precious son. Then I remembered how giving Kris was, and I decided to give them permission to recover his tissue, bones and eyes.

LifeNet Health kept a promise to me that nobody could tell Kris was a donor at the funeral, and they have been by my side ever since I made my decision.

I can look back at this time in my life now, and I can

understand the reservations I felt, but I am so glad I chose to allow my son's body to help others.

I have received two letters from recipients, many invitations from LifeNet Health to celebrate my son's life. They have gifted me with memory books and plaques and kept me informed of how his donation has helped other people.

They gave me other parents to talk to on the donor family website. In so many ways, they had been a God send during my journey of grief.

Here is a copy of the letter I received on Saturday, October 6, 2012 from LifeNet Health.

October 4, 2012

Dear Ms Blythe,

I am writing to follow-up on your request for more information concerning your son's tissue donation. I am pleased to provide you with those results. I hope this information brings some comfort to you and your family.

Tendons and ligaments are used as grafts that repair a torn or ruptured ligament. This surgery allows recipients to resume normal activities with little or no pain and increased range of motion. There have been 11 distributions of this gift for transplantation in the states of California, Pennsylvania, North Carolina, Virginia, Alabama and Washington DC.

The gift of bone typically results in the formation of numerous grafts that are used in various surgical procedures including spinal fusion surgeries in the cervical and lumbar area. Bone grafts are also commonly used in orthopedic surgery to facilitate healing of fractures and for the rebuilding or remodeling of bone in total and partial hip or knee replacements, to repair progressive joint degeneration, and in numerous dental procedures. There have been 27 distributions of this gift for transplant in 13 states throughout the country.

The saphenous vein is a critical implant that is used to save a diabetic from losing their leg. They are also, occasionally, used in coronary bypass surgery. One such graft was distributed to Ohio.

These 39 gifts can improve the quality of life for many people, touching their lives in remarkable ways, and I thank you on behalf of those grateful recipients for Kristopher's and your compassionate acts of love.

If I can be of further assistance to you, please do not hesitate to call or email me.

Sincerely,

Michael Reilly, MA
Donor Family Advocate

The Lion's Medical Eye Bank of Eastern Virginia recovered my son's eyes. Two people received a cornea on the day of Kris's funeral. Today my son's donation lives in a total of 41 people.

It was almost two years before I received my first letter from a recipient. One letter was from a fifteen year old boy who received knee cartilage after he injured a knee in a football accident.

The other letter I received was from a young woman who needed a particular connective tissue for internal surgery. The information about all donations is available from the donor service advocates.

If nothing else has emerged from the traumatic death of my son, I know that he has been a service to many even *after* his death. I know he is patiently waiting for me to join him in paradise someday and paradise has no use for the bodies we leave behind.

The thing I did not know at the time was that my son's giving his gifts to others in need would also be a gift for me; that LifeNet Health would be a strong foundation for me as I entered and walked my journey through grief. I know because of LifeNet Health that I am not alone on this journey. I can trust them to remember Kris—and me.

I want to take this time to thank the kind people at LifeNet Health for their continued support. I want to say *Thank You* to my donor family for sharing their stories and struggles which have aided my continuing recovery. I am grateful for your support and kindness.

A DONOR

I left some gifts when I died

I gave away my tissue, bones and eyes

I will not need them where I will be

It is more important to help someone see

I wish I could have left my heart

But it was too late for that major part

With the gifts I left behind

Some can walk and some can climb

One girl needed tissue for surgery

Another needed a cornea to help her see

I live today in forty four

I pray my gifts will help some more

I am glad I donated my body that day

I would have it no other way

~Renee Hogan Blythe

CHAPTER 23
LOSS AT THE TIME OF BIRTH

● ●

I believe a parent experiences grief whether their baby takes the first breath or not. In fact, I know they do because my niece Leslie lost a child when she was seven months into her pregnancy.

Leslie is a lovely young woman with two other children. She has blue eyes, blonde hair, and she is beautiful. The death of her stillborn infant still lives with her today and I am sure it always will. His name was Hunter.

Leslie told me how she felt when she first realized her baby was dead. She said at first she just wanted to forget it and pretend it never happened at all. She wanted to go home and put it all behind her.

After a few hours, she longed to see her baby and decided she did want to see him. She explained that even though she did look at Hunter, she could not hold him because she knew she could not take him home with her and holding him would mean she could not let him go.

Hunter is at home in his own little pine box with Leslie and the family. She told me that she and her other two children, Gracie and Trevor talk about Hunter often. They have a remembrance day on Hunter's Heaven date, and she has a special box of things that are just for him. Since Hunter's death, she and her husband have a new healthy and happy son. His name is Gage.

Life sends us many hard roads to travel but try to remember the rewards life gives. They are the ones that will help ease the pain.

From the time of conception, I believe we feel love for the unborn child. We experience changes in the body, and we experience the growth of a living being inside of us. The love grows deeper and deeper every single day. The incubation period is nine months, and we anxiously await the arrival by decorating and buying beautiful things for the new creation. The loss of a newborn is just as tragic in many ways as the loss of a child at any age.

Miscarriages in the first trimester of pregnancy are not uncommon occurrences. I have read the body disposes of unhealthy babies, but I do not think we will understand *why* a miscarriage happens until we meet the creator.

I believe pregnancy that goes to almost full term can create the full cycle of grief for mothers. I believe the void in their life is just as real as mine.

I can almost hear the comforting comments a parent who loses a child at birth will hear.

I know that you would not have wanted the baby to live with something was wrong with it.

He or she is with Jesus now.

You will get to see him again someday.

She is God's angel now.

There simply is no words of comfort when a parent loses a baby, a child, a teenager, a young adult or senior citizen. If your baby dies, comfort comes from God and with time.

Leslie kept hearing, *You did not need another child anyway; God has already given you two children.*

I believe mothers also experience grief from abortions. I have had friends tell me, it was some years after an abortion before they felt heart wrenching grief. One friend said, "I think that I was too young to realize the decision I had made at the time, and after I had children and understood how precious they are, I had a lot of guilt about an abortion I had at age sixteen."

Another friend expressed she experienced several years of grief later in life because of an abortion. I have read several articles on this subject, and I believe that any *creation of God is Holy.*

I also believe this all goes back to a destiny here on earth. I believe some babies are here so we can understand loss and the impact it has on life. I am certain there is not one parent in this universe who cannot tell me that they have not had a life lesson in more ways than one, from the death of their child. We get a tremendous lesson on grief.

My suggestion to those who have lost a baby before or at the time of birth is to create a memorial and take time to acknowledge the heaven date every year. Attend Compassionate Friends meetings designed for parents who have lost an infant at birth. Get private counseling if necessary. Make plans to have another baby when the time is right for *you.*

Do not be frightened to have another child. I am fifty six years old and a living witness to many second pregnancies that turned out beautifully. My niece got pregnant again within two months. She planned it. Her baby boy, Gage is healthy with a good set of lungs. They are now a happy family of five.

Most importantly, know in your heart that we are not alone. Others who have experienced miscarriage are willing to talk and help young mothers go on with their life one day at a time.

Stay strong. Jesus is with your baby.

Renee Hogan Blythe

ANGEL OF MY TEARS

How do you love a person
who never got to be,
or try to envision a face
you never got to see?
How do you mourn the death of one
who never got to live
when there is nothing to feel good about
and nothing to forgive?
I love you, my sweet baby,
my companion of the night.
Wandering through my lonely hours,
beautiful and bright.
What does it mean to die before
your born?
To live in the womb of life,
but never see the dawn
Ah! My sweet baby,
who lived like anyone!
Life is a burst of joy and pain.
Until, like yours, it is done.
I love you, my sweet baby,
just as you had lived for years.
No more, no less, do I think of your life,
the Angel of my tears

~Author Unknown.

CHAPTER 24
SUICIDE

•••••••••••••••••••••••••••••••••••

According to The Compassionate Friends Organization, suicide is the third leading cause of death among 10-14 year-olds, the third leading cause among 15-24 year-olds, and the second leading cause among 25-34 year-olds.

A loss due to suicide can be the most difficult losses for a parent to bear. The loss may leave parents with a tremendous burden of guilt, anger and shame. Many parents feel responsible for the death.

Seeking counseling during the first weeks after the suicide is particularly beneficial and advisable. Many parents choose group counseling with other parents who experience the loss of a child to suicide because they can relate with the same feelings.

I have no experience with suicide. So in this chapter I will be sharing a story from a friend who has experienced the death of a child from suicide.

Irma is my dear friend who lives in Florida now. Before she lived there, she and her children lived in Virginia Beach, Virginia.

Just one week ago I had a two day visit from Irma here in Virginia. We talked about my journey and my book most of the time that we were not talking about God.

Irma shared with me the things she lives through from the suicide death of son, Aaron, her middle son at age twenty four. Aaron had never been well accepted by his father due to a divorce during Irma's pregnancy. Although all three of his siblings were from the same parents, he had strong feelings about his father's lack of love for him. He struggled with this most of his life.

On October 29, 1978, Irma found Aaron dead in her attic here in Virginia Beach, Virginia. He shot himself with a pump shotgun. Irma said that many suicides are close to Halloween for some reason.

The first thing Irma wants parents to know is that your child went to Heaven. God loves every one of us the same. *We are all His children. He created us.*

God loves us as we love children and He will never turn His back on His child whether they take their own life, accidentally or intentionally.

So do not listen to preachers who proclaim their *own* hell and brimstone because the Father in Heaven is not full of anger. Irma also encourages parents to look to God for strength.

Guilt and shame are the two most frequent feelings associated with suicide. Parents feel they should have known something was *that wrong* with their child.

Do not be too hard on yourself. We live in a cruel world and children go through a lot of things that parents do not know.

My Kris was fat when he was young. When he was thirteen years old, he wore a size 48 pant and a XXX shirt. Other young people called Kris many names in school even though he had honor grades. He had few friends in school, and I felt fear for him on several occasions in his life.

He finally left school and lost his weight and life got some better for him, but he never quite got over the bullies in school.

Being in love can be devastating to young people. When something goes wrong in a young romance, and the two break-up, many times they simply do not know how to handle it. Many young people feel embarrassment talking about love and relationships with their parents.

Kids have to deal with puberty, broken homes, siblings, grades, teachers, peer pressure and friends. There are so many things they experience that parents cannot help.

Try to find peace and be proud of your child. Be proud of whom your child is within, and the many things they accomplished in their life. If nothing else, they are your child who has your love and God's enduring love.

This is a difficult chapter to write. I pray parents find comfort in a group and take time to talk about your feelings. Remember whether you are to a point of knowing or not, I know your baby is in the arms of Jesus.

Renee Hogan Blythe

TEARS

If tears could build a stairway,

and use memories as a lane,

I'd walk right up to Heaven

and bring my child home again.

No farewell words to be spoken

No time to say goodbye

My child was dead before I knew it

and only God understands the reason why.

My heart still aches in sadness

and secret tears still flow,

what it meant to lose my baby

no one will ever know.

~Author Unknown

CHAPTER 25
LOSS FROM ACCIDENTS

●●●●●●●●●●●●●●●●●●●●●●●●●●●●●●●●

A close friend of mine, Sarah (Liz) has shared her story with me about the tragic death of Kimberly. Kimberly was eighteen years old, a graduate from high school with one year of college behind her and ambitious plans for the future.

She was a beautiful outgoing blonde, full of spirit and with lots of friends. Kimberly and her older sister, Lisa were close.

Kimberly had gone over to see friends one evening on June 26, 1993. On her way home, she lost control of her vehicle and hit a tree which caused the car to catch fire. Mike and Sarah drove up on the wreck and the emergency vehicles. Mike recognized the car, and he ran to it, but it was too late Mike could not even get close to the hot car. Kimberly was dead and badly burned.

This happened to Mike and Sarah over nineteen years ago. They are both still living with the loss of a beautiful daughter in their own unique way.

According to Sarah the hardest part of losing a child by a tragic accident is the *sudden shock*. This is not to mention, the emergency services, ambulances, coroners, police, towing companies, doctors, funeral homes and family a parent must face. In an instant, Sarah and Mike had to start dealing with the thoughts of a beautiful daughter being dead.

Sarah said that she experienced shock, the fog, crushing heart pain, anger and guilt all at the same time. She and Mike sold their home and moved from the area. Sarah said nobody where she now lives knows the *real* Sarah, the real Sarah that will never be again.

Sarah and I were friends for several years before Kris died. I met her in 1993, but even I never got to meet the *real* Sarah. She has shared every grief symptom I have during my journey and then some. I could almost write another book just on her story alone.

I did get to journey with Sarah some in her grief. I can remember one night when we drove down a country road about six years after Kimberly's death, and pulled over to the side of the road and talked for hours.

This was long before Kris died. Sarah needed to talk about Kimberly. I listened, and I tried my best to understand and be understanding, but I had no idea how she felt until June 3, 2008, the day my baby died.

I did experience *shock*. It is an exceptionally hard part of the death process. The morning I walked over to the couch in my living room to wake Kris, I had no idea he was dead. His head tilted to one side, and he looked peaceful as he was sleeping. From the moment, I realized he was dead I started feeling *shock* in the midst of a *fog*.

Candy is a mother from LifeNet Health's donor family who has been kind enough to share her story with me about the tragic loss of her son, Charles at age twenty three.

Charles had two children, Rikku, age three, and Zoey, age five. He had sole custody of the three year old daughter and his five year old daughter was living with his ex-wife.

He was on his way home from work, only about two hundred yards from home when the steering on his vehicle locked due to a manufacturer defect, and he hit a tree. Charles lost his life from the impact.

Candy not only has faced the tragic loss of her baby, but

she now has custody of his three year old daughter. She wanted me to share the six year old is in foster care due to rape by her mother's boyfriend. She got her first visit with her this past weekend.

Charles died on May 13, 2011. Candy is still in early stages of grief. She is experiencing all of the things I have experienced. She is experiencing a difficult time with acceptance and guilt. She has gained weight. She has sleepless nights and long days of crying.

Candy is trying to cope for her precious granddaughter. She has been extremely angry with God. We talked about God and acceptance and guilt and after the conversation she said that she felt better.

Sometimes we just need someone to talk to that understands what we feel. I believe this is vital to the long journey of recovery.

Candy asked me to share that her beautiful grandbabies, her husband Michael, and sons Larry, Will and Harry are the ones who keep her going.

At the end of this chapter, I included a poem written by Charles about two weeks before his death. I am happy to help Candy get her baby's poem in print for taking the time to share with me.

Donna and John Coster also shared with me about their son Adam. Adam died in a car accident trying to avoid a deer on October 9, 2011. Today is October 7, 2012. I can almost feel the pain the Coster family is feeling right now on the first anniversary of Adam's Heaven date. Donna explained that the poem titled *When Tomorrow Starts Without Me* speaks volumes about her feelings. There was a reading of this poem at Adam's funeral.

This is Dana's Story. Dana is also a member of LifeNet Heath's group.

It was not that knock on the door in the middle of a Friday or Saturday night that every parent of a teen or young adult fears. The call came to me at work on December 21, 2011, a rainy Wednesday afternoon.

We had just celebrated Matt's 28th birthday two days before, and we were anticipating Christmas celebrations with family. All was right with the world when I left the house that morning. I remember looking back as I went out the front door and thinking *I'm blessed.*

Joey, my 17 old was asleep in his bed. Matt was asleep on the couch, safe and sound. He worked at night and slept through the day, but this week he was on vacation. He had moved back in with us about a year before.

My cell phone rang at 1:00 p.m. It was an incoming call from Joey. This was no surprise he and his brother called me every day around that time —usually to see if I wanted to take them out for lunch or the usual question, "What's for supper?" But this time, Joey just calmly said, "Mom, there are two state troopers here, it is about Matt, and they need you to come home right now."

Somehow, I went into robot mode. I just said, "I'll be right there."

I went over and told my friend. She and I talked about the joys and worries of the kids all of the time, and she said "Just leave everything, go!" Like a zombie, I drove home in the gloomy rain behind a slow car.

I just kept telling myself, this cannot be what I think it could be. He must just be in trouble, maybe on the wet roads he slid into another car or something and got scared and did not stop, so now they are looking for him. When I pulled into my driveway and saw the two trooper cars and saw them standing on the porch, I knew.

It happens a lot like people see it on TV. They asked me to come in and sit down. I remember telling Joey, "You do not have to be here for this honey."

Looking back, I think he grew up in that moment. He came and sat down beside me and said he wanted to stay. They told me that Matt was in a car accident earlier that day and that *he did not make it.* Those words should never be spoken about your child.

They handed me his wallet. That wallet stayed clutched in my hand day and night for the first couple of days and stayed under my pillow for months. It somehow kept me connected. Most say that those first days are a blur, but for me, I remember every single thing that happened that day, every word spoken, every food dish that came in, every phone call, every last detail as it was yesterday.

I find peace knowing that Matt lost his life instantly. He never had to suffer, never had to be afraid. I never had to make that choice like some parents do to take away the life support. I never had to feel the dread of knowing that my child was terminally ill.

I find peace in knowing that his eyes and tissues have helped someone else. It was like God had just reached out of the sky and picked him up. Seeing him for the last time, he looked like he had simply gone to sleep.

Although he is not what I call *showy religious,* I know my son's heart and his spirit. If he is not in Heaven, then I honestly know of no one else that will be.

The last thing that Joey remembers about his brother as he walked out of the door that morning is Matt feeding the neighbor's cat. He watched him call the cat over to see a red cardinal that was by the window. We later learned that many believe that seeing a cardinal right before or after a death symbolizes a safe passage into the afterlife.

Although most days I am okay, I am never great—never complete. My grief has changed a lot during this first year. I know no other words to describe the first months except sheer terror, anxiety, sleepless nights and exhaustion. I had anger, but it was short-lived. It was no one's fault.

To say that it was not fair would be to imply that it should have happened to someone else and that I wish on no one.

Many parents share their experiences and say the second year of grief is worse than the first year of grief. I believe that is true as the one year anniversary of my son's death approaches. I feel the shock has worn off, and the reality is setting in my heart.

My oldest son is dead, too far ahead, for far too long; my youngest son feels the same pain that I do. I am getting selfish with my grief. I feel as it is my walk alone. Only another parent who has lost a child can truly understand these feelings.

I know that many care and can only imagine, but they can never fully know. I know that before this happened to me, I did not truly understand.

Grief comes in waves still, sweeps over your heart out of nowhere. For days, I fought just to breathe, just to stay afloat. I have read many grief books and like most, researched the internet for as much grief literature as I can digest.

One parent described it best for me. She said that after losing her son she walked along the side of a massive black abyss, and knew that, at any given moment, she could slip and fall inside and never come back. She also said that even ten years later, she is still highly aware that the abyss exists, but she does not feel that she is walking as close to the edge.

I go on because I'm *still blessed* with a wonderful son. Life has already cheated him out of his only brother, his best friend. I refuse to cheat him out of a mother. I go on because I realize God needed him for some reason. He had given him to me at Christmas, and He took him back at Christmas.

I go on because I have twenty eight years of memories to treasure. I go on because I know that Matt would not expect it any other way. He was a realist, easy going, laid back, and loved.

I can sometimes still feel his presence, his oneness with nature. Joey and I were talking about Matt one day, and I said to him, "Can you imagine Matt talking to Jesus face to face?"

Joey's reply was, "What an ingenious pair."

Now, what more could a parent ask for when honoring

your loved one? I hope we can all find peace until we see the children again.

After I read Dana's story I could see we all feel the same feelings, the ones of us who are so unfortunate to know the feelings of losing a child.

She spoke of hanging on to her son's wallet. It reminded me of when the police officer handed me Kris's driver's license. A policeman had asked for his identification when they came to the house that morning, and when he handed it back to me, I held it in my hand for the rest of that day, and I carry it in my wallet to this day.

For several years, I would pull out Kris's driver's license and show people whom he was when I would be talking about him. Now I have some scanned pictures on my cell phone. It is funny how we feel and react in the same way about children.

Here is a message from Nina.

I am Chito's Mom, Nina. I live in Round Rock, Texas— originally from Plano, Texas. Chito died one week after his 24th birthday. Born on Valentine's Day in 1985, Chito crossed over on February 21, 2009. He died in a car accident.

Chito is my middle child, and he left a daughter behind, who is now ten years old. I have encountered some instances where people say, "It's been over a year, you should be *over it* by now." This is *far* from the truth.

Nina has shared some poems and a picture of her son that readers can find at the end of this chapter.

One year is only the beginning for most any parent who has lost a child. This relates to the understanding people give us when we are feeling the crushing pain inside day after day. Until they experience the death of a child themselves, they will never understand there is no way to get over it.

Accidental shootings have got to be one of the most difficult losses. The guilt from a child getting a gun and accidentally shooting their self has got to be a terrible thing to live and comprehend. To those parents I say please spend as much time as possible with God. He will give comfort. Remember God knows a parent never means for that to happen and deep inside the parent knows it too.

I believe whether we lose a child by a tragic car accident, a drowning, a fall, an accidental shooting, by murder, or for any other reason or in any way we immediately go to *a place of no return*.

This place can be a seriously scary place to live in a day after grueling day. It is a place where we begin facing every sinful thought and every mistake we have made during an entire lifetime. It is a place that seems unusually cold and empty. The place of no return gives us unhealthy habits and changes us for life in many ways.

It takes a part of us as we mourn the death of a child. It becomes a place we get accustomed to living in and sometimes we stay in this *place of no return* much longer than we should stay.

One thing that I do know now is that as horrible as this place is, it does have mercy, and it will let us out if we take the first step to turn the handle and open the door.

Once we make the decision to get out of the *place of no return* healing can begin, and we can start creating a *new normal*. My prayers are with grieving parents every day, every step of the way.

POEM BY CHARLES FERGUSON

Under the moon, filled with pain,

Stands a boy stripped of pride and filled with guilt.

He shouts, "Where are you"

He hears nothing.

When he looks thru the mist of agony, he sees only shame.

He walks up to a lonely lake, only to see what he longs for.

A sweet sacrifice, too sweet for any man is the reason the lake remains lonely.

He asks, "Are you her?"

The lake replies, "Aye sir, I am for what you seek".

He submerges into the lake and feels the warmth of love, at last…

The lonely sweet sacrifice finds love

And the young man, finds his pride, loses his guilt, and feels no more pain

Dedicated to Nina and Chito

BELIEVE

I believe you are in a better place

I can't believe I'm still here

I believe that one day I will smile

I believe that you are

I can't believe how hard it is not to touch you

I believe you touched many

I can't believe how sad I am

I believe you are so in peace

I can't believe all that weep

I do believe you are in my heart forever to keep

nmfp 03-11-09 In Loving Memory

CHITO

A MOTHER NEEDS NO REMINDERS

I need no reminder of how you made me laugh

Or how angry I'd get

I need no reminder of how much I love you

I need no reminder of how much I miss you

I need no reminder of how you came to be

Nor of one on how you parted from me

I silently pray every day- my inner soul wails with sadness

A Mother needs no reminders

A Mother lives and breathes for her children

nmfp 06-13-09 RIP RFL My Lifetime Valentine

CHAPTER 26
MURDER

●●●●●●●●●●●●●●●●●●●●●●●●●●●●●●●●●●●●

I want to start by sharing some information from *Hope of Life* [homicide, which is the, 15th leading cause of death. It can be justifiable or excusable depending upon the circumstance and not every homicide is a crime such as killing someone in self-defense or a hunting accident. Murder, however, is a criminal homicide.

On average, sixteen people between the ages of ten and twenty four lose their life by murder each day in the U.S. An estimated 15,241 people died from murder nationwide in 2009.

Of female murder victims, 35% experience murder by an intimate partner. Also, in 2009, 521 workplace homicides occurred in the U.S. In 2008, there were 11,773 alcohol-impaired driving fatalities.]

The anger associated with the murder of your child can become overwhelming. Many parents find that the majority of people are uncomfortable listening or talking about homicide.

My personal belief is that most people only think it happens to other people. Some people think it only happens to *sinful* people. Unfortunately, homicide knows no boundaries. People of all races, religions, and creeds feel the effects of homicide. Bad things happen to *good* people every single day.

Most parents of a murdered child become involved in courtroom experiences and must re-live the details of the death of their child that is—if the killer becomes charged with the offense. Some parents, like a close friend of mine, find themselves in front of parole boards every few years to keep the person who killed their child in prison.

When the family gets some justice and satisfaction with the killer behind bars, the fact still remains their baby is dead forever. Nothing changes that... *Nothing*.

Many families live with fear and terror and a tremendous amount of suffering their child endured by the hands of another human being. They live with what they know, seldom sharing it. They experience fear of murder for their other children or their spouse.

This reminds me of a movie about a couple who both had AIDS. In the movie, the man said, "At birth, there is a silent clock that begins ticking, and at that very second we start dying."

He went on to say, "When a doctor tells us that we are going to die that silent clock becomes a loud ticking clock, and we *realize* we are dying."

I believe it is a lot the same for a family that experiences losing a child to murder. They *realize* it can happen any day to anyone.

God gives the commandment *Thou Shalt Not Kill* for a reason. The unbearable pain murder causes Him, family and friends are only three of them. It does not matter if it is murder by a gun, knife, poison, drowning or accidental murder. Murder kills the spirit of the living too many times.

I was not sure if this should be the chapter I included military deaths in but to me war is murder in many ways. To the parents of the brave soldiers who defend this country in this cold hateful world we live in, I would like to say, "I am sorry for your loss." It must be heart-breaking. I have talked to so many veterans who cannot love God because of all of the destruction they have witnessed. Try to take comfort in knowing your baby is with Jesus and safe from harm today. I would like personally to say, *thank you* for your sacrifice. My heart aches for the many parents who have suffered this loss.

I know in my heart where a parent must find comfort, and that my friend is with the help of the Heavenly Father.

Take one day at a time, one step at a time, say the Lord's Prayer and remember the best of times with your child. Memories *are* forever.

Try to find a good group through your local hospital, the military, hospice or elsewhere in the community.

Talk to God, He listens. One of the most essential steps is creating a *new normal* so we can start making new friends and keep living a healthy life.

Your clock *is* ticking. One day parents will be in a beautiful paradise with their children when their destiny is complete here on earth. One day we *will* find peace.

THINKING OF YOU WITH LOVE

We thought of you with love today, but that is nothing new.
We thought about you yesterday
and days before that too.
We think of you in silence
we often speak your name.
All we have are memories
and your picture in a frame.
Your memory is a keepsake
with which we will never part.
God has your soul in His keeping
we have your memories in the heart.
A million times we have wanted you.
A million times we have cried.
If love could have saved you,
Your body would have never died.
It broke our hearts to lose you.
Your spirit did not go alone.
For a part of us went with you...
The day God called His baby home.

~Author Unknown

CHAPTER 27
SIDS

● ●

My step daughter, Star lost a child to SIDS in 1992. Star is a six foot tall blonde with dark brown eyes and slender, but shapely figure. She was only eighteen when she gave birth to Amber.

Amber was a beautiful, healthy baby girl just learning to walk and talk. Star had gone to the grocery and left Amber sleeping in the care of her husband, Chris.

Star left for about two hours, and when she returned the baby was still asleep. She questioned her husband, and he said he had checked on her about forty five minutes earlier, and she was sleeping.

When Star checked on Amber, she was blue and unresponsive. Amber had died and gone to heaven. In the blink of an eye, the world as we know it can come tumbling down with no warning.

Next, Star dealt with the ambulances, coroners, police and long interrogations over the death of her precious child. Star spent many hours under interrogation with the police and so did Chris because they were young nineteen year old parents.

The final determination from the autopsy was SIDS or Sudden Infant Death Syndrome which alleviated any guilt by either party. However, Star told me that because of the intensive questioning the police had put them through she had experienced a lot of doubt in her mind about her husband's role in the death of her baby.

Unfortunately, SIDS remains a significant cause of death in infants under one year old. Thousands of babies die of SIDS in the United States each year. SIDS is most likely to occur between two and four months of age. SIDS affects boys more often than girls. Most SIDS deaths occur in the winter.

The cause of SIDS is unknown. Many doctors and researchers now believe that SIDS could be caused by several different factors, including problems with the baby's ability to wake up (sleep arousal); the inability for the baby's body to detect a buildup of carbon dioxide in the blood and other medical conditions.

I believe it all goes back to destiny, and only the Father in Heaven knows the reason why. The unbearable truth is most doctors and researchers do not fully understand SIDS. The loss of a baby in this way is a truly heart wrenching experience for any parent.

I was with Star for most of the time she went through visitation, the funeral and the ceremony at the cemetery. She would sit and stare. She said she just walked around in a fog for weeks and weeks looking for her precious baby. She had to deal with going home and seeing all of her toys and clothes and bottles and things Amber loved. She longed deeply for her baby in her arms. Sadness became over-whelming, and she had to seek professional counseling. Her marriage ended with Chris and eventually she moved away from Richmond, Virginia.

Since Amber's death Star has given birth to four more beautiful babies that are almost grown now, but she has never forgotten Amber for one minute. She told me just last year she still has many moments she longs to hold Amber in her arms. This feeling can be referred to as *empty arms syndrome*.

I feel parents of a SIDS child experience all of the emotions I experienced when I found Kris dead at age thirty. There was no warning. He worked the day of his death painting a house and came home and cooked dinner. He was in a good mood with no signs of illness. In fact, there was no illness. Kris was disease free. His heart simply stopped in his sleep. It was like my friend said—SIDS at age thirty.

Some people believe it is harder to lose a child after they have spent many years together; others believe it is harder to lose a baby starting a new life. I believe that there is *no harder than* when it comes to the death of a child.

When a parent loses a child for any reason, at any age, it is a terrible event that happens in your life and one that will never be forgotten.

I want you to know that with the help of others who have experienced loss, prayers to the heavenly Father and with time, you can begin to heal and start living a *new normal.*

There is no right way and no wrong way to grieve, and there is no time limit. All of the feelings you experience on the long journey of grief are remarkably *normal.*

We all struggle just the same way and we continue to live it one day at a time until we finally begin to feel better. Read, get out and visit family and friends, go to group, stay busy—all of these things will help even when it does not feel like it. *Keep looking up.*

LITTLE ANGELS

When God calls little children
to dwell with Him above.
We mortals sometimes question
the wisdom of His love.

For no heartache compares
With the death of one small child,
Creating all the memories
That is loving and mild.

Perhaps God tires of calling
the aged to His fold.
So He picks a small rosebud
before it can grow.

God knows how much we need them
So He takes only a few,
to make the clouds of Heaven
more beautiful to view.

Believing this is difficult
still somehow we must try.
The saddest word mankind will know
Will always be, "Goodbye".

So when a child departs
we who stay behind,
must realize God loves children,
Angels are hard to find.

~Author Unknown

CHAPTER 28
THE BROKEN SPIRIT

●●●●●●●●●●●●●●●●●●●●●●●●●●●●●●●

I believe the spirit is that part of you that makes you breathe, blink your eyes and feel things. It is *us*. It is inside us. All humans have a spirit. When we die, it leaves your body because, without it, we are dead.

I read the human spirit is a component of human philosophy, psychology and religion - the spiritual or mental part of humanity. The human spirit is the mental functions of awareness, insight, understanding, judgment and other reasoning powers.

I believe the human spirit should soar with happiness. This is the way God intended it. The spirit of a human is always searching for what is perfect, for harmony, for peace, cognition and realization, for knowledge, wisdom, truth and beauty, for love and especially for truth concerning the true Creator all of these are of eternal duration.

The death of a child will certainly break the human spirit. I know I have been there and had it happen to me.

A broken spirit places a wonder into something for which there is no logical explanation. Suddenly, I found myself unable to think clearly, unable to smile, unable to enjoy the beauty and unable to love. I became bitter and saddened. It felt as though a part of me died.

For a long time, I attributed this to the death of my son. I would say when Kris died part of me died with him. In some ways, this is true. Now I realize a great deal of the feeling I had was due to my *broken spirit.*

As I studied my Bible and continued to read self-help books and spiritual books, my spirit began to heal slowly. I now believe the human spirit has a connection to God through the *silver cord.* I believe we have a lifeline to the Father in Heaven just as *the cord* lifeline we have with children.

Wisdom is an essential, tremendous power. It is the *light.* Wherever light shines, darkness and ignorance vanish.

Wisdom is a characteristic of the created spirit and the spiritual mind, and it has within itself the qualities of happiness, truth, knowledge, balance, beauty, harmony, and peace.

However, wisdom is characteristic of a human who has recognized the existence of his spirit and cooperates along with the spiritual laws of God. Wisdom is using spiritual knowledge and force.

With the tool of wisdom, I have been able to heal my broken spirit. I now have *joy.* Joy comes from your spirit. I can feel joyous that my precious son in the arms of the Heavenly Father. I can feel joy that someday I will join him. I can feel love from God. I can finally love and feel joy again.

A human who is full of love is also rich in wisdom, and a human who is rich in wisdom is also full of love.

Growth within love and wisdom teaches the human spirit to recognize God. First, however, the human spirit must learn the truth, and thereby will gain freedom and peace—peace that is imperishable and a power without an end.

I know this seems deep, but it is simple. *Learn to love like God loves.*

So many parents I have spoken with over the past few years have broken spirits. Many of them have anger with God because of the loss of their child. For those who have this anger, I beg you to reconsider and realize that *God is Love. God is Kind.*

God is forgiving. He is the One that will bring your heart peace and give comfort to your mind and spirit.

I do understand how parents feel when they feel broken with anger. This is normal. For five years, I have been searching answers to why. Why did my baby have to die? I believe I will get the answer someday when I go back home.

For today, I choose to believe it is not for me to know *why* but to know Kris is safe and in a *good place* waiting for me. I choose to believe everything happens for a reason even when we do not understand it. I choose to believe that God has a brilliant plan for all of us.

At the end of my book, readers will find a list of some reading materials I have used to help me along the way in my personal journey of grief. I found comfort in some of the things I read. I found disbelief in some. After I read them all, things slowly came together to bring me the peace I feel today, and *my spirit can soar again* at last.

THIS IS BEAUTIFUL

She jumped up as soon as she saw the surgeon come out of the operating room. She said: 'How is my little boy? Is he going to be alright? When can I see him?'

The surgeon said, 'I'm sorry. We did all we could do, but your boy did not make it.'

Sally said, 'Why do little children get cancer? Does God care anymore? Where were you, God, when my son needed you?

The surgeon asked, 'Do you need some time alone with your son? One of the nurses will be out in a few minutes before we transport him to the university. Sally asked the nurse to stay with her while she said good bye to her son. She ran her fingers lovingly through his thick red curly hair. 'Would you like a lock of his hair?' the nurse asked. Sally nodded yes. The nurse cut a lock of the boy's hair, put it in a plastic bag and handed it to Sally.

The mother said, 'It was Jimmy's idea to donate his body to the University for Study. He said it might help somebody else. 'I said no at first, but Jimmy said, 'Mom, I will not be using it after I die. Maybe it will help some other little boy spend one more day with his Mom.' She went on, 'My Jimmy had a heart of gold; Always thinking of someone else. He always wanted to help others when he could help.

Sally walked out of Children's Mercy Hospital for the last time, after spending most of the last six months there. She put the bag with Jimmy's belongings on the seat beside her in the car. The drive home was difficult. It was even harder to enter the empty house. She carried Jimmy's belongings, and the plastic bag with the lock of his hair to her son's room. She started placing the model cars and other personal things back in his room exactly where he had always kept them. She lay down across his bed and, hugging his pillow, cried herself to sleep.

It was around midnight when Sally awoke. Lying beside her on the bed was a folded letter. The letter said:

'*Dear Mom,*

I know you are going to miss me, but do not think that I will ever forget you, or stop loving you, just 'cause I'm not around to say 'I Love You'. I will always love you, Mom, even more with each day.

Someday we will see each other again. Until then, if you want to adopt a little boy so you will not be so lonely, that is okay with me. He can have my room, and old stuff to play with. If you decide to get a girl instead; she probably would not like the same things us boys do. You will have to buy her dolls and stuff girls like you know.

Do not be sad thinking about me. This is a neat place. Grandma and Grandpa met me as soon as I got here and showed me around some, but it will take a long time to see everything. The angels are so cool. I love to watch them fly. And, you know what? Jesus does not look like any of his pictures. Yet, when I saw Him, I knew it was Him.

Jesus himself took me to see GOD! And guess what, Mom? I got to sit on God's knee and talk to Him as I was somebody important. That is when I told Him that I wanted to write you a letter to tell you good bye and everything. I already knew that was not allowed.

Well you know what Mom? God handed me some paper and His own personal pen to write you this letter I think Gabriel is the name of the angel who is going to drop this letter off to you.

God said for me to give you the answer to one of the questions you asked Him where was He when I needed him?' 'God said He was in the same place with me, as when His son Jesus was on the cross. He was right there as He always is with all His children.

Oh, by the way, Mom, no one else can see what I've written except you. To everyone else this is just a blank piece of paper. Is that cool?

I have to give God His pen back now He needs it to write some more names in the Book of Life. Tonight I get to sit at the table with Jesus for supper. I'm sure the food will be great.

Oh, I almost forgot to tell you. I do not hurt anymore. The cancer is all gone. I'm glad because I could not stand that pain anymore and God could not stand to see me hurt so much, either. That is when He sent The Angel of Mercy to get me.

The Angel said I was a Special Delivery! How about that?

Signed with Love from God, Jesus & Me

CHAPTER 29
THE HEALING

● ●

Before I get into this chapter of my book, I would like to acknowledge that it was over four years before my healing began. I think your healing can begin sooner than mine with better information.

After spending four long years in total depression and shutdown, I began to notice some changes. I could go for a day or two without crying. I could laugh without feeling guilty. I could make plans and keep them. There were many times I planned a typical trip to grocery shop and just could not make myself go because of depression.

I also had a difficult time keeping engagements with people. I would just choose not to go. This was so out of context for me. I have always been a person ready to go do anything.

Once I realized some changes were beginning to happen to me, I tried to concentrate on them more. I made a conscious effort to, *not cry*. I began to think about fun times with Kris and I would try to laugh more often. I began to get out of the house more and visit people. I *tried* to start living again.

A week later, I found myself crying all day again and wondering why when things were getting better. I believe now that Satan was using his power to hold me down.

As long as Satan had me in a *lost state of mind* he was happy.

Satan had won. So next, I started ordering Satan out of my house and screaming at God for not listening to me when I was begging Him for help. This went on for several months.

I just could not believe that God would not help me. I spent time every morning reading my Bible. I watched Shepherd's Chapel at 6:00 a.m. I watched Joyce Meyers Ministries at 8:00 a.m. I watched Joel Osteen on Sunday morning, and I spent time with God each day in prayer and meditation.

And then one day God said, *"Get up and do something, nothing will ever change unless you make an effort."* That is all He said, but I knew it was God saying it without any doubt. So I did what I thought He was asking and started making plans for a different future.

After about two weeks, God said to me *"What about your book?"* I thought to myself, "My book! That is what God wants me to do."

I had planned to write a book in real early stages of grief and even started writing one, but soon realized I was not ready for it. So here is my book, parents are reading it today.

I will have to say reliving my journey has been exceedingly difficult for me. I have re-lived my entire experience since the death of my son. I have a concern that I am not saying the right things to other grieving parents. I have done the research and asked for help from several people. Now, when it is all said and done, I do feel much better.

I just want parents to know this is my personal journey and what I have experienced and what a few others have shared with me. Some may be on a totally different path than me. I only pray some of the things parents can relate too and get some help in their grief journey from my sharing.

I think there has been a lot of healing in writing about my journey of grief. I can look back and see many of the emotions I had along the way, and look at them in a different way than I perceived them when I was living them.

Now, I can understand why I had the feelings I did, and choose never to go back to that *place,* again.

Today I have a future. Today I can smile and feel good about it. Today I can make plans and keep them. I am finally a *new me.*

Do not get me wrong, it is a *new me,* but it is also a *me* that I can live with and hopefully share with others.

I just want parents to know that there is a way to heal from the crushing pain in your heart. I know all too well what mothers are experiencing. It is so normal to feel lost when your child dies.

I realize that even with a family to look after, parents can feel isolated inside because nobody understands. *Time* does heal, but *time* has no limit, and *time* has no mercy.

Today, I need to remind everyone once again to repeat the *Lord's Prayer* at least once per day. Think of something funny and laugh as often as possible. Laugh even if your only means of laughing is watching the same funny video over and over. Laughter keeps us well.

Do not overeat or not eat. Take time for *Yourself.* By that, I mean take time to talk to God or take a walk or go to a movie, a park, to see a friend or go somewhere that feels comfortable. Go and get a haircut, get your nails done or buy yourself something new.

Also, read your Bible. If reading the Bible is too hard at first, buy a good spiritual book, or a book on grief like your reading right now. Do what God told me to do, *"Do something."*

I am not trying to prescribe a cure. I am only sharing things that have helped me during my journey of grief.

If only one person gets some knowledge from my journey, I will feel blessed. Just yesterday, my Mom said, "I am afraid if your book is not popular it will set you back, and you will get depressed again."

"Mom, I promise never to go back to that dark and lonely place again." I said.

My healing has begun. It is not complete. I still cry. I still miss my son. I still deal with change. However, I can say I am so much better today than last year that I could never let myself go back there again. I will continue to follow my journey, and I will continue *Looking Up!*

Hopefully, in the next five years I can write a sequel to *When Your Baby Dies* and give parents more insight on where this journey of grief has taken me from here. Until then, I will sit still and listen. Remember, *God is with all of us.*

Renee Hogan Blythe

HEALING

My child died

My insides crumble

My heart is sore

My spirit humble

For too long, I have cried

Ached so bad and prayed to die

Lift me up dear God

Help me heal

I need your love more than anytime now

My child has gone; my head is bowed

Take my hand and lead the way

My life is yours for one more day

CHAPTER 30
THE NEW NORMAL

• •

When a child dies life changes forever, things will never be normal again. Chapter 12 talks about the change. What we must learn to get healthy again is how to create for ourselves a *new normal*.

When I heard about a new normal for the first time, I thought how do I create a new normal? That made no sense to me. There was certainly nothing normal about my life in my state of mind or about my life now with Kris gone, but I found myself asking, "What is a new normal?"

Finally, I started thinking about my teen years and moving out on my own away from my parents house. I remembered that I had created a new normal at that time. I remembered the birth of Kris and the new normal that created for me.

This is when I realized what I must do and how I must go about it. I started working on my own *new normal* after the death of my only child.

Now let's talk about how? For over thirty years, the first thought on my mind when I awoke was Kris. This happened from the day of his birth. The day he died did not end that first thought of him. In fact, Kris is still the first thought on my mind every morning.

Of all of the changes I have made, this is the hardest one to change. Now, instead of waking, thinking of Kris and crying, I wake, think of Kris and feel comfort in knowing he is safe in the arms of Jesus. This is the only difference but it is a *new normal* for me.

Instead of buying his favorite food at the grocery, I buy *my* favorite food or buy his favorite food and enjoy it for him. Instead of watching the door waiting for him to come in from work every day, I keep myself busy between the hours of 5 and 6 p.m.

Instead of buying Kris presents on his birthday or Christmas as I did for so many years, I buy a memory ornament for the tree and a decoration for home. Instead of crying, I try to laugh. Instead of screaming, I read my Bible.

Instead of eating the fantastic meals Kris would cook for me, I make his recipes. I have found a way to talk about Kris with joy in my voice instead of tears in my eyes.

I have learned to feel close to Kris I only have to speak out loud to him. I spend my days doing things we enjoyed doing together and finding new things to do alone.

I have found a new appreciation for people again. I have hope for my future, and I live one day at a time. My *new normal* is okay. It is much different, but it is okay.

I feel this new normal is one I can share with people and one I can use to make new friends. It is a normal that can still be *me* without Kris. The most valuable thing I want to share is the *new normal* I have created has room to grow and get better and better every day.

I know how grieving parents feel things will never be normal again. It is normal to feel that way because it is *true*. Things will *never* be the same (or normal) again.

We must learn to speak differently, spend time with family differently, be among friends differently, clean differently, do laundry differently, cook differently, buy differently and even expect differently.

Every holiday is now different. Every Christmas, every

Easter, every birthday, every Mother's Day or Father's Day, every Valentine's Day, it does not matter Memorial Day is different now. We even have one more date to remember, and that is the *Heaven date*. Please believe me when I say that I understand.

Learning to live a *new normal* is not easy but necessary to progress during your journey of grief. Right now, there is an opportunity to make some significant changes in your life. Try to make good changes... changes that feel good.

We should take the time that we devoted to the child that has died, and give that time to ourselves or to your other children and spouse. Take the time to make life better today.

I am taking one day at a time and looking up instead of down. I try to remember the good things and forget the hurtful things. My future looks brighter today than it has looked in a terribly long time. I know my dream come true is out there, I just have to help to make it happen.

If I could say anything other than I understand to the people who take the time to read my book I would say, "It *is* true things do get *softer*."

I do not think there is any set time on when that will happen for us, but I know in my heart that it *will*. Time does have a way in helping us to heal.

I would also like to say to the daddy's who have lost a child that it is okay to cry. I understand men like to be strong and keep the family together, but sometimes even your wife and children need to see daddy cry. It is okay. Try not to keep everything bottled up.

I have exciting plans for my *new normal*. I plan to live my remaining years happy. I plan to make the dreams that never came true, come true. I hope to devote time to helping others who need someone to talk to during their journey of grief. I have plans to write another book. I want to look at today with hope and expectation of good things to come.

I cannot begin to tell parents the weight that has lifted from my heart over the past year. I can breathe again, thanks to my *new normal*. So can others.

I have mentioned several times throughout my book about the journey of grief. It is a *journey* we all travel differently in your *own unique way*. Now, let me mention this, *life is also a journey*.

I believe none of us know what life's journey holds for us or why hurtful things have to happen to us, but I have often said, "If I can survive the death of my only child, I can survive anything." *Bring life on!*

The death of a child is a struggle from the moment it happens. It is a struggle no parent should live. When I look back at my life today, I can finally see my life coming to full circle, and I truly believe everything happens for a reason. It is just like my Kris told me, "You'll understand someday Mom."

My book is complete, but my journey has not ended. I still have a lot of feelings I deal with on a day to day basis. I think the difference now is I do know that God is with me, and He is helping me heal. I *know* there is a reason I am still among the living.

May God bless every grieving parent and may He carry us when we cannot get up, pick us up when we fall and give us strength when we feel we have none. Amen.

God does love you and your baby.

NEWS FROM THE AUTHOR

●●●●●●●●●●●●●●●●●●●●●●●●●●●●●●●

I have good news! I finally had my dream of Kris. Here is my dream.

I had the walls in my home freshly painted. I was happy because the house looked so clean and my home was beginning to feel like home again. Janet came to visit me. I gave her a tour showing off my newly painted rooms. I said to Janet, "The walls looked better when Kris painted them the last time."

Later, I went to sleep and when I woke up I walked from my paneled bedroom into the kitchen. I found myself in shock when I saw that Kris had painted words all over my newly painted walls!

On my kitchen cabinets in capital letters and red paint was "KRIS WAS HERE!" On my dining room wall he painted in blue, "I love you!"

I was extremely curious to see the rest of the house. I went into the living room and in black paint over the fireplace it read, "You Said I Would Not Visit!" I walked to Kris's bedroom, and he left the message, "I MISS YOU MOM!" Next, I looked in my office and in green on my new yellow wall he wrote, "ONLY JOKING!"

I remember feeling confused, happy and mad all at the same time, and I woke up.

This is not the dream I have envisioned. I thought my

dream would be about me and Kris walking through Heaven together with him showing me around and spending the day together. However, my Kris had to let me know that he is still around. He is still the same Kris.

Finding My New Normal

They tell me, I must learn to live a new normal
But I'm not sure that I know how
There is nothing about my life that is normal
Not yesterday…not now.

Each morning I wake crying
Feeling totally down and blue
Is this the new normal they are talking?
Is this my lifetime New?

I try to go on living
I try to hide the pain
This new normal is not working
How can they say these things?

Each day I miss my baby more
With every single breath
There is nothing normal about this pain
Or the memories of his death

A new normal I can understand
It does make sense to me
But learning to live a new normal
Is not done so easily

Please tell me how to do this thing
Place a new normal in my life
I need to learn how right now
To be a good mother and a good wife

I will take each day as it comes
One day at a time
And when my new normal finds me
I pray my normal will feel like mine

~Renee Hogan Blythe – 2013

SUGGESTED READING MATERIALS

●●●●●●●●●●●●●●●●●●●●●●●●●●●●●●●●

This is a list of the books I have read. Some of them helped me a lot and some helped me a little, but they all gave me something, especially the Holy Bible.

King James Version *The Holy Bible*. New York Bible Society: 1999

Eadie Betty J. *Embraced by the Light*. Detroit: Gold Leaf, 1992

Sylvia Brown *Exploring the Levels of Creation*. Hayhouse, November 2007

Dannion Brinkley *Saved by the Light*. Harper Paperbacks, 1994

Sylvia Brown *Book of Angels*. HayHouse: 2003

William P. Young *The Shack*. Windblown Media: 2007

Charles Stanley *The Source of My Strength*. Thomas King Inc: 1994

Joyce Meyer *Help Me! I'm Depressed.* Harrison House, Inc.:1998

Joyce Meyer *Living Beyond Your Feelings* Faith Words Hachette Book Group: 2011

Joyce Meyer *Never Give Up!* Faith Words Hachette Book Group: 2008

Sylvia Brown *Life on the Other Side.* New American Library, a Division of Penguin Putnam Inc.: 2000

Julianne Maclean *The Color of Heaven.* Julianne Maclean: 2011

Elizabeth B. Brown *Surviving the Loss of a Child.* Revell, a division of Baker Publishing Group: 1988

Don Piper *90 Minutes in Heaven.* Revell, a division of Baker Publishing Group: 2004

Sam Parnia, M.D. *What Happens When We Die?* Hay House: 2006

Cherie Hill *Waiting On God.* Cherie Hill: 2012

Christine Brooks Martin *Pray What God Says.* Morris Publishing: 2010

David Tuffey *Being Happy.* Altoria Publications: 2011

Quiet Moments With God for Women. David C. Cook: 2002

REFERENCES

I have compiled a list of reference websites parents can go to for help. Your local Hospice or local hospital can give information on groups for grieving parents. For parents who have lost a child from murder, suicide or tragic accident, a group can help. Below is the list of websites.

Grieving Moms Healing Together
Join this Closed Group on Facebook

Grieving Mothers
Join a closed grieving mothers group on Facebook.
http://www.grieving-mothers.org

The Compassionate Friends
http://www.compassionatefriends.org

Forum for Grieving Parents
http://forum3.aimoo.com/forumforgrievingparents

Cancer.Net
http://www.cancer.net/coping/grief-and-bereavement/grieving-loss-child

Grieving Parents
http://www.GrievingParents.com

Babies With Wings
http://www.babieswithwings.com

Healing The Spirit
http://www.healingthespirit.org/support-groups.php

Bereaved Parents of the USA
http://www.bereavedparentsusa.org

ACKNOWLEDGEMENTS

●●●●●●●●●●●●●●●●●●●●●●●●●●●●●●●●●●●

My greatest admiration and love goes out to my Mother, Linda Stewart Hogan. Thank you for bringing me into this world so Kris could be born and I could have thirty wonderful years being a mom to him. Thank you for the hours you have devoted to me on the telephone and listened to me cry. I love you so very much.

I am thankful to Irma Appleton, my dear friend who has helped me become a more spiritual person through her continued dedication to God, to me and to Kris, and for sharing her story with me about the death of her son from suicide.

I want to thank Leslie Hogan, my niece for sharing her story about the loss of her baby at birth and for being the sweet person she has become as a young adult and mother.

A sincere thank you goes to Sarah "Liz" Petrey for the many hours she spent with me on the telephone and in person sharing in my grief and her own. I would like to thank you Liz, for your continued friendship and for allowing me to include your story of Kimberly in my book.

I also want to thank my donor family friends, Dana Hiles, Donna and John Coster, Candy Ferguson, Nina Lopez Goldsberry, and Michael Reilly for sharing their poems and stories and helping me with the Loss from Accidents and Donor Family chapters.

I would like to say thank you to Sandra Flaathen, Doris Susko, Barbara Been, J Laney, Janet Franks and to Bobby Plummer for being my friends when I thought I had none. You all mean so much to me.

A special thank you goes out to my brothers Tim Hogan and Tony Hogan and their families, and to Sylvia Brooks and her family for being at my side during one of the most tragic experiences in my life.

A heartfelt thank you goes to my long time friend, Byron Howard for helping me with my book.

I also want to thank the Gravatt family for being there so many times when I felt alone.

Finally, I would like to thank Frank Gravatt and Greg Laney for being my friends and putting up with my long journey of grief for the past five years. Both of them have been by my side, paid my bills and let me have the time I have personally needed to grieve and to heal. You will always hold a special place in my heart forever. I love you, both.

IN MEMORY OF

KRISTOPHER GLEN HARDRICK

DECEMBER 15, 1977 – JUNE 3, 2008

RENEE & ROBERT

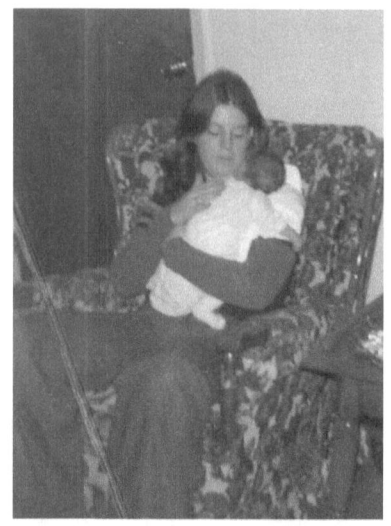

MOTHER & BABY

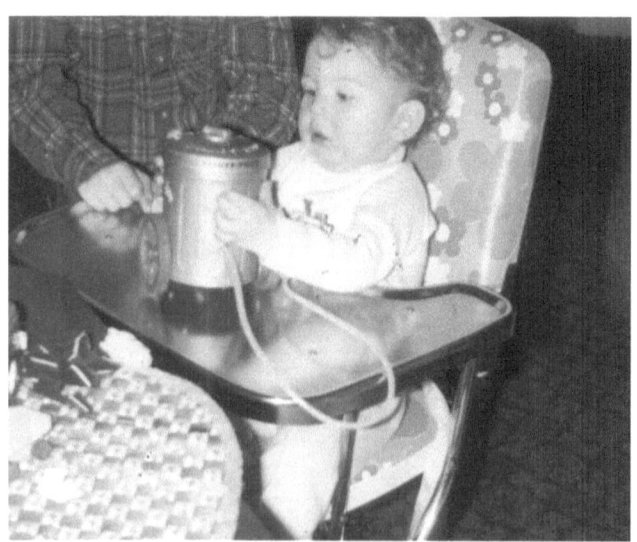

FIRST BIRTHDAY

RENEE & KRIS AGE 1

KRIS 18 MONTHS

KRIS AGE 2

KRIS AGE 3

KRIS AGE 6

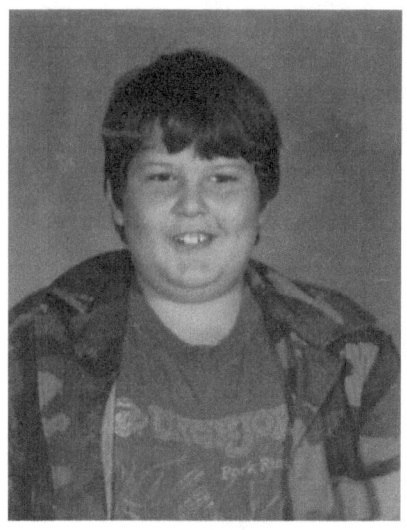

KRIS AGE 10

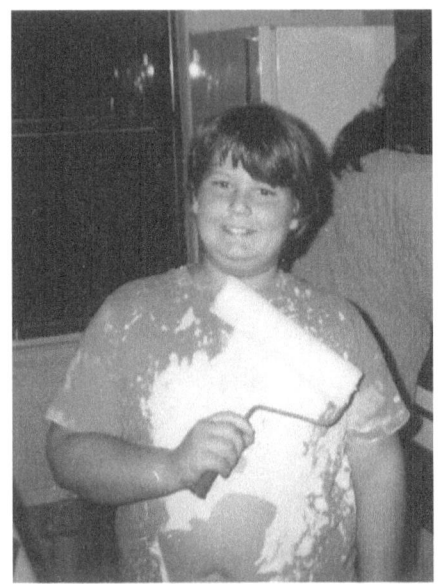

KRIS AGE 11

KRIS AGE 12

KRIS & PAPAW

KRIS & ZIGGY

KRIS AGE 13

KRIS AGE 14

KRIS AGE 15

KRIS AGE 20

KRIS & MOM

CHRISTMAS AT MA'S

KRIS AT 27

KRIS & MARJO FRIENDS

KRIS & PATTY

NOTES

NOTES

NOTES